OPPOSING
VIEWPOINTS®
SERIES

Oil

Other Books of Related Interest:

Opposing Viewpoints Series

America in the Twenty-First Century

Cars in America

Conserving the Environment

Energy Alternatives

The Environment

Global Resources

Iraq

Population

Current Controversies Series

Alternative Energy Sources

Conserving the Environment

The Middle East

War

At Issue Series

Foreign Oil Dependence

How Should America's Wilderness Be Managed?

Is the World Heading Toward an Energy Crisis?

What Sources of Energy Should Be Pursued?

"Congress shall make
no law ... abridging
the freedom of speech,
or of the press."

First Amendment to the U.S. Constitution

The basic foundation of our democracy is the First Amendment guarantee of freedom of expression. The Opposing Viewpoints Series is dedicated to the concept of this basic freedom and the idea that it is more important to practice it than to enshrine it.

OPPOSING
VIEWPOINTS®
SERIES

Oil

Andrea C. Nakaya, Book Editor

GREENHAVEN PRESS
An imprint of Thomson Gale, a part of The Thomson Corporation

THOMSON
™
GALE

Detroit • New York • San Francisco • San Diego • New Haven, Conn.
Waterville, Maine • London • Munich

Bonnie Szumski, *Publisher*
Helen Cothran, *Managing Editor*

© 2006 Thomson Gale, a part of The Thomson Corporation.

Thomson and Star Logo are trademarks and Gale and Greenhaven Press are registered trademarks used herein under license.

For more information, contact:
Greenhaven Press
27500 Drake Rd.
Farmington Hills, MI 48331-3535
Or you can visit our Internet site at http://www.gale.com

LIBRARY OF CONGRESS CATALOGING-IN-PUBLICATION DATA

Oil / Andrea C. Nakaya, book editor.
   p. cm. -- (Opposing viewpoints)
  Includes bibliographical references and index.
  0-7377-3328-4 (pbk. : alk. paper) 0-7377-3327-6 (lib. bdg. : alk. paper)
  1. Petroleum reserves. 2. Petroleum industry and trade. 3. Energy consumption.
I. Nakaya, Andrea C., 1976– II. Opposing viewpoints series (Unnumbered)
  HD9565.O55 2006
  338.2'7282--dc22
                                   2005054541

Printed in the United States of America
10 9 8 7 6 5 4 3 2 1

Contents

Chapter 3: What Energy Policies Should America Pursue?

Chapter 4: How Does Oil Impact International Relations?

Why Consider Opposing Viewpoints?

> *"The only way in which a human being can make some approach to knowing the whole of a subject is by hearing what can be said about it by persons of every variety of opinion and studying all modes in which it can be looked at by every character of mind. No wise man ever acquired his wisdom in any mode but this."*
>
> *John Stuart Mill*

In our media-intensive culture it is not difficult to find differing opinions. Thousands of newspapers and magazines and dozens of radio and television talk shows resound with differing points of view. The difficulty lies in deciding which opinion to agree with and which "experts" seem the most credible. The more inundated we become with differing opinions and claims, the more essential it is to hone critical reading and thinking skills to evaluate these ideas. Opposing Viewpoints books address this problem directly by presenting stimulating debates that can be used to enhance and teach these skills. The varied opinions contained in each book examine many different aspects of a single issue. While examining these conveniently edited opposing views, readers can develop critical thinking skills such as the ability to compare and contrast authors' credibility, facts, argumentation styles, use of persuasive techniques, and other stylistic tools. In short, the Opposing Viewpoints Series is an ideal way to attain the higher-level thinking and reading skills so essential in a culture of diverse and contradictory opinions.

In addition to providing a tool for critical thinking, Opposing Viewpoints books challenge readers to question their own strongly held opinions and assumptions. Most people form their opinions on the basis of upbringing, peer pressure, and personal, cultural, or professional bias. By reading carefully balanced opposing views, readers must directly confront new ideas as well as the opinions of those with whom they disagree. This is not to simplistically argue that everyone who reads opposing views will—or should—change his or her opinion. Instead, the series enhances readers' understanding of their own views by encouraging confrontation with opposing ideas. Careful examination of others' views can lead to the readers' understanding of the logical inconsistencies in their own opinions, perspective on why they hold an opinion, and the consideration of the possibility that their opinion requires further evaluation.

Evaluating Other Opinions

To ensure that this type of examination occurs, Opposing Viewpoints books present all types of opinions. Prominent spokespeople on different sides of each issue as well as well-known professionals from many disciplines challenge the reader. An additional goal of the series is to provide a forum for other, less known, or even unpopular viewpoints. The opinion of an ordinary person who has had to make the decision to cut off life support from a terminally ill relative, for example, may be just as valuable and provide just as much insight as a medical ethicist's professional opinion. The editors have two additional purposes in including these less known views. One, the editors encourage readers to respect others' opinions—even when not enhanced by professional credibility. It is only by reading or listening to and objectively evaluating others' ideas that one can determine whether they are worthy of consideration. Two, the inclusion of such viewpoints encourages the important critical thinking skill of objectively evaluating an author's credentials and bias. This evaluation will illuminate an author's reasons for taking a particular stance on an issue and will aid in readers' evaluation of the author's ideas.

It is our hope that these books will give readers a deeper understanding of the issues debated and an appreciation of the complexity of even seemingly simple issues when good and honest people disagree. This awareness is particularly important in a democratic society such as ours in which people enter into public debate to determine the common good. Those with whom one disagrees should not be regarded as enemies but rather as people whose views deserve careful examination and may shed light on one's own.

Thomas Jefferson once said that "difference of opinion leads to inquiry, and inquiry to truth." Jefferson, a broadly educated man, argued that "if a nation expects to be ignorant and free . . . it expects what never was and never will be." As individuals and as a nation, it is imperative that we consider the opinions of others and examine them with skill and discernment. The Opposing Viewpoints Series is intended to help readers achieve this goal.

David L. Bender and Bruno Leone,
Founders

Introduction

"What else is out there? This is a question for the world's entire energy supply system. For surely, somewhere, the unexpected is brooding, and waiting to happen."

—*Daniel Yergin,*
chairman of Cambridge
Energy Research Associates

In September 2005 two major hurricanes hit the Central Gulf Coast of the United States causing devastating damage and flooding and displacing thousands of residents. Hurricanes Katrina and Rita also impacted many offshore oil rigs, refineries, and pipelines, which were either temporarily shut down in anticipation of the storm, or forced to shut down because of storm damage. The consequence of this reduced oil supply was higher gas prices across the nation. The United States and many other countries are heavily dependent on oil for their energy needs. As events surrounding these hurricanes reveal, any disruption to the oil supply system has a significant impact. By looking at the consequences of hurricanes Katrina and Rita, the significance of the oil supply system to both the United States and other countries becomes clear.

As economic growth increases around the globe, nations are demanding steadily increasing amounts of oil. The International Energy Agency estimates that global demand for oil is at 83.5 million barrels a day, an increase of nearly 20 percent from a decade ago. The United States accounts for approximately a quarter of that demand. However, while the world's demand for oil has grown rapidly, its ability to extract and refine oil has grown less quickly. U.S. energy officials estimate that currently the world can only produce 900,000 to 1.4

million barrels a day more than it already pumps. According to the Petroleum Industry Research Foundation, while global demand for oil is expected to grow by nearly 2 million barrels a day in 2005, the world's capacity to refine and process crude oil is expected to grow by less than half that. These numbers mean that when the oil supply in one part of the world is disrupted, it is becoming increasingly difficult to compensate by getting it from somewhere else.

As a result of this tightening of supply, any disruption to the supply and distribution system can have significant consequences, as revealed by the 2005 hurricanes. A considerable portion of America's oil comes from the U.S. Gulf region. According to the *Wall Street Journal*, the region accounts for 28 percent of domestic oil production. In addition, 10 percent of U.S. imports flow through that region, and many refineries are located there. Thus, when Katrina and Rita struck the area, temporarily halting oil production, refining, and transport, U.S. oil supplies were significantly reduced. According to a report by the U.S. Energy Information Administration (EIA), Katrina initially reduced oil supplies by 1.4 million barrels a day. While some production resumed following the hurricanes, many experts predict that full recovery will be slow.

In response to the reduced oil supply, nationwide gas prices immediately increased. According to the EIA, the national average price for a gallon of regular unleaded gasoline rose to a record $3.07 on September 5. In some southeastern states it temporarily went higher than $5 per gallon. Most analysts predict that as a result of the hurricanes, prices will stay high for the near future. According to Phil Flynn, senior market analyst for Alaron Trading Corporation, "People will have to get used to higher prices for a while."

Many analysts believe that the hurricanes' impact on gas prices proves that world demand for oil is outpacing supply. *Washington Post* writer Justin Blum argues that while in the past an event such as a hurricane would not have had a significant effect on oil prices, the nature of the market has changed that. According to Blum, "Surging global demand—coupled with production and refining that have not kept pace—virtually wiped away spare capacity that could be tapped if operations halted in some part of the world." Many experts predict a future where oil prices are highly vulnerable to world events. Robert J. Lieber, professor of government and international affairs at Georgetown University explains why. "When the market is running tight, anything—whether it's a hurricane, or war, or revolution, or terrorism—can precipitate a crisis," he says. Stephen Leeb, author of *The Oil Factor*, echoes Lieber. "This is a horribly tight market," he asserts. "Maybe even I'm not worried enough."

Others contend that the real problem is big oil companies, which have failed to invest in finding new oil supplies and building new refineries. According to a September 2005 *Wall Street Journal* article, oil producers are earning more today than ever before. Journalist Derrick Jackson finds that "of the world's seven most profitable corporations, four are [oil companies] ExxonMobil, Royal Dutch Shell, BP, and Chevron. ExxonMobil is the world's most profitable company, making $25.3 billion [in 2004]." Journalist Art Perlo believes that these companies do not make investments to increase the oil supply because when there is an oil shortage as the result of an emergency, they can simply raise their prices and make more money. Says Perlo, "There is more profit for the oil industry when it is *not* prepared for disaster." Critics of big oil charge that in the case of hurricanes Katrina and Rita, increased oil prices were simply adding to the huge profits these companies already make. In Jackson's opinion, "Big oil looted the nation." He adds, "Stay fixated, if you wish, on the thieves and desperate families who are [looting stores in New Orleans]. . . . But ExxonMobil and big oil are looting the nation, and no one is declaring martial law on them."

In addition to debating who or what is to blame for high oil prices, most people wonder what lies ahead as the world demands more and more oil. The authors of *Opposing Viewpoints: Oil* explore this question in the following chapters: Is There an Oil Crisis? How Can America Reduce Domestic Oil Prices? What Energy Policies Should America Pursue? and How Does Oil Impact International Relations? Oil supplies are vital to the survival of billions of people around the globe, fueling transportation, food production, heating, and manufacturing. The implications of price increases and shortages are thus extremely important. As David Goodstein, professor at the California Institute of Technology predicts, "Civilization as we know it will come to an end ... when the fuel runs out."

OPPOSING
VIEWPOINTS®
SERIES

Is There an Oil Crisis?

Chapter Preface

At a 1956 meeting of the American Petroleum Institute, American geophysicist M. King Hubbert introduced a theory that would have a tremendous impact on subsequent discussions about the state of worldwide oil supplies. Known as the Hubbert peak theory, this theory states that because oil is a nonrenewable resource, at some point there will be a peak in its production, followed by declining production. Hubbert predicted that oil production would peak between 1965 and 1970 in the United States, and worldwide in 2000. U.S. oil production did peak in 1971. Most experts believe, however, that the worldwide production peak has not yet occurred. World economies are extremely dependent on oil, therefore questions about how much is left, and how long it will last, are of great concern for nations around the world. However, there is heated debate over whether or not a peak and a depletion will occur, as predicted by Hubbert.

Proponents of Hubbert's theory believe that although worldwide supplies did not peak in 2000, that peak is approaching in the very near future. As energy investment banker Matthew R. Simmons explains, "Oil and gas resources are basically nonrenewable and so someday they will basically run out." Kenneth S. Deffeyes, professor of geology at Princeton University states, "Global oil production will probably reach a peak during this decade [2001–2010]. After the peak, the world's production of crude oil will fall, never to rise again."

Critics of Hubbert's theory contend that there is no imminent oil peak. They point to the fact that the world continues to find new technology for discovering and extracting oil. Robert Bradley, president of the Institute for Energy Research in Houston, Texas, points out, "Despite a century of doom and gloom about the imminent depletion of fossil-fuel reserves, fossil-fuel availability has been increasing even in the face of record consumption." According to Professor David Deming, "We have not run out of oil because new technologies increase the amount of recoverable oil, and market prices—which signal scarcity—encourage new exploration and development. Rather than ending, the Oil Age has barely begun."

Whether or not the world faces an oil crisis remains a controversial topic with important implications for an oil-dependent world. The authors in the following chapter offer various answers to this much-debated question.

> *"[Oil shortages will lead to] economic recession and a crumbling stock market."*

A Worldwide Oil Shortage Is Approaching

Colin J. Campbell

In the following viewpoint Colin J. Campbell examines worldwide oil discoveries and depletions that occurred in the twentieth century. He concludes that despite new discoveries and advances in drilling technology, the world's oil supplies are limited and will run out in the near future. He believes that the world has refused to face up to this reality and warns that it must begin planning for this approaching crisis. Campbell is a geologist and the author of numerous articles about the world's oil supply.

As you read, consider the following questions:

1. According to Campbell, how have advances in technology and operating efficiency impacted production peaks for many new oil fields?

2. Why will it be impossible for the United States to maintain its rate of oil imports, as argued by the author?

3. By how much must the United States cut its yearly oil demand, in Campbell's opinion?

Colin J. Campbell, "Peak Oil: A Turning Point for Mankind," *Social Contract*, vol. XV, Spring 2005, pp. 180–82. Copyright © 2005 by Social Contract Press. Reproduced by permission.

The fundamental driver of the 20th century's economic prosperity has been an abundant supply of cheap oil. At first, it came largely from the United States as it opened up its extensive territories with dynamic capitalism and technological prowess. But U.S. discovery peaked around 1930, which inevitably led to a corresponding peak in production some 40 years later

Oil Discoveries

The focus of supply then shifted to the Middle East, as its vast resources were tapped by the international companies. They, however, soon lost their control in a series of expropriations as the host governments sought a greater share of the proceeds. In 1973, some Middle East governments used their control of oil as a weapon in their conflict with Israel's occupation of Palestine, giving rise to the "first oil shock" that rocked the world.

The international companies, anticipating these pressures, had successfully diversified their supply before the shock, bringing in new productive provinces in Alaska, the North Sea, Africa and elsewhere. These deposits were more difficult and costly to exploit, but production was rapidly stepped up when control of the traditional sources was lost. In part that was made possible by great technological advances in everything from seismic surveys to drilling. Geochemistry and better geological understanding made it possible to identify the productive trends, once the essential data had been gathered. The new knowledge showed both where oil was and where it was not, reducing the scope for good surprises.

The industry found and produced the expensive and difficult oil from the new provinces at the maximum rate possible, leaving the control of the abundant, cheap, and easy oil in the hands of the Middle East OPEC [Organization of the Petroleum Exporting Countries] countries. The latter were accordingly forced into a swing role, making up the difference between world demand and what the other countries could produce. It was contrary to normal economic practice and concealed the gradual impact of depletion, growing shortage, and rising cost, which would otherwise have alerted us to what was happening.

Depletion

But these new provinces faced the same depletion pattern that had already been demonstrated in the United States. The larger fields, which are found and exploited first, gave a natural discovery peak. Advances in technology and operating efficiency also reduced the time lag from discovery to the corresponding production peaks. Whereas it took the United States 40 years, the North Sea, which is now at peak, did it in just 27 years.

As discovery in the accessible areas dwindled to about one-quarter of consumption, the industry, which fully appreciated this obvious link between discovery and production, turned its attention to the last remaining frontier, namely the ocean depths. It is axiomatic that no one would look for oil in 6,000 feet of water if there were any easier places left. The deepwater domain is also subject to depletion with an even shorter time lag between the peaks of discovery and production. Although much of the ocean is deep, only a few areas have the essential geology, giving a potential of not more than about 85 Gb (billion barrels)—enough to supply the world for less than four years. It is no panacea.

Price Falls

A combination of circumstances led to a dramatic fall in the price of oil in 1998. These included unseasonably warm weather; an Asian recession that reduced the demand for swing Middle East production; the collapse of the ruble [Russian currency]; encouraging exports; overestimation of supply by the International Energy Agency (IEA), which misled OPEC; and further turns in Iraq. Furthermore, there were motives to

Analysis of Major Oil Producing Countries, 1993–2003

Year	Countries w/ Output Declining	Countries w/ Output Increasing	Countries Past Peak	Countries Peaking in Year
1993	18	30	17	1
1994	11	37	18	0
1995	14	34	18	2
1996	14	34	20	1
1997	11	37	21	1
1998	20	28	22	2
1999	23	25	24	3
2000	16	32	27	1
2001	29	19	28	3
2002	27	21	31	0
2003	22	26	31	0

SOURCE: John Attarian, *Social Contract*, Winter 2004/2005.

talk down the long-term price of oil as oil companies and their financial advisers planned acquisitions. Major companies, plainly seeing that exploration could no longer underpin their future, took the opportunity of the price crisis to merge, successfully concealing their real predicament from the stock market. Budgets were slashed and staffs purged in a climate of uncertainty leading to an improvident draw on stocks.

The OPEC countries themselves did everything possible to foster the notion that they could flood the world with cheap oil at the flick of a switch. It was a strategy aimed to inhibit investments in natural gas, non-conventional oil, renewable energy or energy saving that they feared might undermine the market for their oil, on which they utterly depend.

A Trend of High Oil Prices

But it was a short-lived price collapse. Before long, the underlying resource and depletion pressures manifested themselves again with prices rebounding in a staggering 300 percent increase in 12 months, when another anomalous fall occurred at the end of 2000. It was partly triggered by profit taking for year-end financial reporting and partly by the hope of a brief reprieve as spring demand traditionally falls.

The underlying trend is due to reassert itself, leading to the resumption of soaring oil prices. The Middle East is working flat out to try to offset the decline of its old fields. In large measure, new production in Venezuela can come only from in-fill drilling in old heavy oil fields, which is dependent on the amount of effort and investment. . . . Its oilmen speak of reduced capacity.

The market may hope that some important recent discoveries tell a different story with a happier ending. The long-known Azadegan prospect on the Iraq-Iran border was at last tested, delivering some 5 Gb of reserves to Iran. Kashagan East in the north Caspian [Sea] found about 7 Gb of high sulfur oil at great depth, demonstrating that the prospect was not one huge structure as hoped, but several independent reefs. The disappointment caused two major companies to withdraw from the venture.

Promising deepwater finds continue to be made off West Africa, but it is becoming clear from the experience of the Gulf of Mexico that deepwater operations do test technology and management to the absolute limit. Small accidents or setbacks can have devastating consequences in this extreme environment. Petroconsultants recently announced the total oil discovery for 2000 at 11.2 Gb, less than half consumption, and of that much was in the former Soviet Union and in deep water off West Africa.

A Coming Crisis

The reality is that there is no real reprieve. Gradually the market—and not just the oil market—will come to realize that OPEC can no longer single-handedly manage depletion. It will be a dreadful realization because it means that there is no ceiling to oil price other than from falling demand. That in turn spells economic recession and a crumbling stock market, the first signs of which are already being felt.

The United States is perhaps the most vulnerable to the coming crisis having farther to fall after the boom years, which themselves were largely driven by foreign debt and inward investment. The growing shortfall in oil supply since its own peak of production was made good by soaring oil imports, now contributing more than half its needs, and a move to natural gas. The rate of import cannot, however, be maintained as other countries pass their own production peaks, putting ever more pressure on the Middle East. The North Sea is now at peak, with the United Kingdom being off 7 percent in 2000 and 16 percent off from October to October, meaning that production is set to fall by one-half in ten years. For every barrel imported into the United States, there will be one less left for anyone else, a situation inevitably leading to international tensions. . . .

The U.S. has to somehow find a way to cut its demand by at least 5 percent a year. It won't be easy, but as the octogenarian said of old age, "the alternative is even worse." Europe faces the same predicament as North Sea production plummets. Although it may draw on gas from Russia, North Africa and the Middle East to see it over the transition, assuming that new pipelines can be built in time, that creates a new and unwelcome geopolitical dependency.

All of this is so incredibly obvious, being clearly revealed by even the simplest analysis of discovery and production trends. The inexplicable part is our great reluctance to look reality in the face and at least make some plans for what promises to be one of the greatest economic and political discontinuities of all time. Time is of the essence. It is later than you think.

> *"When will the world's supply of oil be*
> *exhausted? ... Never."*

There Is No Approaching Oil Shortage

M.A. Adelman

Worldwide oil supplies are not nearing depletion, maintains M.A. Adelman in the following viewpoint. Adelman believes that extraction methods will continue to improve, and that reserves will turn out to be much larger than current estimates. In his opinion, fears of an impending oil crisis are the result of actions by the Organization of the Petroleum Exporting Countries (OPEC), which fixes prices and output, resulting in panic over the supply of oil. Adelman is professor emeritus of economics at the Massachusetts Institute of Technology and author of several books, including The Genie Out of the Bottle: World Oil Since 1970.

As you read, consider the following questions:

1. What influences the definition of "proved reserves," according to the author?
2. Adelman states that at the end of 1970, non-OPEC countries had about two hundred billion barrels of oil in proved reserves; what does he say their reserves are now?

M.A. Adelman, "The Real Oil Problem," *Regulation*, vol. 27, Spring 2004, pp. 16–21.

3. According to the author, why will OPEC never cut output in the future?

According to "conventional wisdom," humanity's need for oil cannot be met and a gap will soon emerge between demand and supply. That gap will broaden as the economies of Europe, Japan, and several emerging nations grow and increase their energy needs. The United States is at the mercy of Middle Eastern exporters who can use the "oil weapon" to cripple the U.S. economy. Unless we increase domestic oil production radically or cut consumption, or nations like Russia quickly exploit recently discovered oil fields, the United States will find itself in an oil crisis.

But conventional wisdom "knows" many things that are not true. There is not, and never has been, an oil crisis or gap. Oil reserves are not dwindling. The Middle East does not have and has never had any "oil weapon." How fast Russian oil output grows is of minor but real interest. How much goes to the United States or Europe or Japan—or anywhere else, for that matter—is of no interest because it has no effect on prices we pay nor on the security of supply.

The real problem we face over oil dates from after 1970: a strong but clumsy monopoly of mostly Middle Eastern exporters cooperating as OPEC [Organization of the Petroleum Exporting Countries]. The biggest exporters have acted in concert to limit supply and thus raise oil's price—possibly too high even for their own good. . . .

Is Oil Running Out?

Oil is not the first fossil fuel that conventional wisdom has identified as nearing exhaustion. Even before 1800, the worry in Europe was that coal—the supposed foundation of their greatness—would run out. European production actually did peak in 1913, and is nearly negligible today. Is that the result of exhaustion? Hardly—there are billions of tons in the ground in Europe. But it would cost too much for the Europeans to dig it out. At a price that would cover cost, there is no demand. Hence, the billions of tons of European coal are worthless and untouched. The amount of a mineral that is in the ground has no meaning apart from its cost of extraction and the demand for it.

In 1875, John Strong Newberry, the chief geologist of the state of Ohio, predicted that the supply of oil would soon run out. The alarm has been sounded repeatedly in the many decades since. In 1973, State Department analyst James Akins, then the chief U.S. policymaker on oil, published "The Oil Crisis: This Time the Wolf Is Here," in which he called for more domestic production and for improved relations with oil-producing nations in the Middle East. In 1979, President Jimmy Carter, echoing a CIA [Central Intelligence Agency] assessment, said that oil wells "were drying up all over the world." Just last year [2003], the *New York Times* reported that "oil reserves are expected to dwindle in the decades ahead," while the International Energy Agency forecasted that oil output will grow in the Persian Gulf between now and 2030, but it will decline elsewhere.

The doomsday predictions have all proved false. In 2003, world oil production was 4,400 times greater than it was in Newberry's day, but the price per unit was probably lower. Oil reserves and production even outside the Middle East are greater today than they were when Akins claimed the wolf was here. World output of oil is up a quarter since Carter's "drying up" pronouncement, but Middle East exports peaked in 1976–77.

Despite all those facts, the predictions of doom keep on coming.

The Real Oil Crisis

The true crisis (or whatever it is) started in 1973–74 when a dozen mostly Middle Eastern nations mutually agreed to cut

The Impact of Technology

Technology is a continuous process, enabling discovery and production from places and by means unimaginable in the past. The most famous of oil-supply pessimists, M. King Hubbert, predicted correctly in 1956 that U.S. oil production would peak in 1970 and then rapidly decline. But the oil potential in the deep Gulf of Mexico and in Alaska and the impact of a host of technology developments assured continued U.S. oil development. Hubbert necessarily ignored all these factors, because he based his projections only on history.

Arlie M. Skov, Issues in Science and Technology, *Summer 2005.*

their output. They have been constraining production ever since. They lock away and sterilize the cheapest oil in the world to raise the price and their revenues. . . .

When Will the Oil Run Out?

It is commonly asked, when will the world's supply of oil be exhausted? The best one-word answer: Never. Since the human race began to use minerals, there has been eternal struggle—stingy nature versus inquisitive mankind. The payoff is the price of the mineral, and mankind has won big, so far.

However, alarmists point to world oil prices and claim that what has happened "so far" will not continue much longer. They might have a point—if the world oil market featured several different, competitive suppliers. But instead, it is dominated by a monopoly supplier, so the higher prices in themselves mean nothing. To understand this, one needs a quick course in resource economics.

Minerals are produced from reserves, which are mineral deposits discovered and identified as able to be extracted profitably. Are oil reserves dwindling? Is it getting harder to find or create them? Conventional wisdom says: Of course. But once again, conventional wisdom is wrong.

Reserves are a type of warehouse inventory, the result of investment. One cannot make a decision to drill and operate an oil well without a forecast of the well's production. Moreover, as the well's output falls over time with decreasing pressure, the unit operating cost of the well's output will rise. When the operating cost rises above the price that the oil will fetch in the marketplace, the well will be shut down. Whatever oil is left underground is not worth producing, given current prices and technology. The well's proved reserves are the forecast cumulative profitable output, not the total amount of oil that is believed to be in the ground.

In the United States and a few other countries, a nation's "proved reserves" is the programmed cumulative output from existing and pending wells. In other countries, the definition of "reserves" varies, and the number is often worthless. At its best (e.g., the estimates released by the U.S. Geological Survey), the "probable reserve" is an estimate of what will eventually be produced in a given area, out of existing and new wells, with current technique and knowledge, and at prevailing prices.

Ultimate Knowledge?

But the size of "known reserves" is not an adequate forecast of eventual production, unless we assume that in oil, as in Kansas City, "they've gone about as far as they can go."[1] Watching [the movie musical] "Oklahoma!" we smile at those who actually believe this—and we should likewise smile at those who think they know how much oil will be extracted from a well or in an area. To predict ultimate reserves, we need an accurate prediction of future science and technology. To know ul-

1. As settlers moved West across the United States in the 1800s, some people believed that further exploration was not possible—that they had gone as far as they could go.

timate reserves, we must first have ultimate knowledge. Nobody knows this, and nobody should pretend to know.

The dwindling of reserves is a legend firmly believed because it seems so obvious. Assume any number for the size of reserves. From it, subtract a few years' current output. The conclusion is absolutely sure: Reserves are dwindling; the wolf is getting closer. In time, production must cease. Oil in the ground becomes constantly more valuable—so much so that a gap forms between how much oil we want and how much we are able to afford because of scarcity. Civilization cannot continue without oil, so something must be done.

And indeed, in some times and places the oil does run down. Output in the Appalachian United States had peaked by 1900, and output in Texas peaked in 1972. But the "running out" vision never works globally. At the end of 1970, non-OPEC countries had about 200 billion [barrels] remaining in proved reserves. In the next 33 years, those countries produced 460 billion barrels and now have 209 billion "remaining." The producers kept using up their inventory, at a rate of about seven percent per year, and then replacing it. The OPEC countries started with about 412 billion in proved reserves, produced 307 billion, and now have about 819 billion left. Their reserve numbers are shaky, but clearly they had—and have—a lot more inventory than they used up. Saudi Arabia alone has over 80 known fields and exploits only nine. Of course, there are many more fields, known and unknown. The Saudis do not invest to discover, develop, and produce more oil because more production would bring down world prices.

Growing knowledge lowers cost, unlocks new deposits in existing areas, and opens new areas for discovery. In 1950, there was no offshore oil production; it was highly "unconventional" oil. Some 25 years later, offshore wells were being drilled in water 1,000 feet deep. And 25 years after that, oil-men were drilling in water 10,000 feet deep—once technological advancement enabled them to drill without the costly steel structure that had earlier made deep-water drilling too expensive. Today, a third of all U.S. oil production comes from offshore wells. Given current knowledge and technique, the U.S. Geological Survey predicts offshore oil will ultimately comprise 50 percent of U.S. production.

The offshore reserves did not just happen to come along in time. In an old Mae West movie, an admirer of one of her rings declared, "Goodness, what a diamond!" She coldly replied, "Goodness had nothing to do with it." Likewise, offshore production did not begin and develop by providence or chance, but only when new knowledge made investment profitable. And the high potential economic rewards were a powerful inducement for the development of the new knowledge. Offshore drillers found a new way to tap oil beneath the deep ocean. Oilmen in Canada and Venezuela discovered how to extract oil from those nations' oil sand deposits. As new techniques decreased the cost of extraction, some of the oil slowly began to be booked into reserves.

New Reserves

Worldwide, is it getting harder and more expensive to find new deposits and develop them into reserves? Up to about 15 years ago, the cost data clearly said no. Since then, much of the relevant data are no longer published.

To make up for that lack, [researcher] Campbell Watkins and I tabulated the sales value of proved reserves sold in-ground in the United States. Our results are a window on the value of oil reserves anywhere in which entrepreneurs can freely invest. (That rules out the OPEC countries and a few more.) If the cost of finding and developing new reserves were increasing, the value per barrel of already-developed reserves would rise with it. Over the period 1982–2002, we found no sign of that.

Think of it this way: Anyone could make a bet on rising in-ground values—borrow money to buy and hold a barrel of oil for later sale. With ultimate reserves decreasing every year, the value of oil still in the ground should grow yearly. The investor's gain on holding the oil should be at least enough to offset the borrowing cost plus risk. In fact, we find that holding the oil would draw a negative return even before allowing for risk.

To sum up: There is no indication that non-OPEC oil is getting more expensive to find and develop. Statements about non-OPEC nations' "dwindling reserves" are meaningless or wrong. . . .

The World Monopoly

The oil "crisis" started in 1971–1973 when a dozen producer nations agreed to raise oil prices by cutting their output. They continue that cooperation today. Their cost of expanding output, which is mostly the return on the needed investment, is a small fraction of the price that they charge for oil. . . .

OPEC is a forum whose members meet from time to time to reach decisions on price or on output. Fixing either one determines the other. There have in effect been several OPEC cartels since the countries first banded together more than three decades ago. The members re-constitute the cartel as needed to meet current problems.

In every oil price upheaval, there has been persistent excess capacity (which could not happen under competitive pricing). Even if we started with zero excess, every output reduction itself creates excess capacity among the OPEC countries. They refrain from expanding output in order to raise prices and profits. Recently, we have heard high prices explained by low inventories. That is true—the cartel cuts production, which lowers inventories, which raises prices. Because each member's cost is far below the price, output could expand many fold if each producer followed its own interest to expand output, which would lower prices and revenues. Only group action can restrain each one from expanding output. . . .

Price fixing by private companies on the OPEC scale would not be tolerated in any industrial country. In the United States, the officers of firms that engage in such activities go to jail. But the OPEC members are sovereign states, subject to no country's laws. Moreover, the United States and other nations want to think they have the OPEC nations' support—particularly the Saudis.

This alleged support consists in "access" to oil. But in a global market filled with buyers and sellers, everyone has access. Another myth is mutual obligation: The OPEC nations supply oil, the United States protects them. In truth there is no choice; we must protect the OPEC nations from outsiders or neighbors. They owe us nothing for protection and will give us nothing. Of course, OPEC will supply oil. The only question is how much oil—and that determines the price. The supposed OPEC (or Saudi) obligation to supply is what lawyers call "void for vagueness." But those in government crave assurance that they are accomplishing something, and they will pay for that assurance. . . .

The cartel members supposedly cooperating with us . . . are committed to nothing. They will raise or lower output to increase their profits. There is and will be no shortage; they are glad to produce the amount they have themselves decided. They will never cut off output in the future, any more than in the past—it would cost them money.

> "We may have a lot less time than we
> thought to replace [oil] with something
> cleaner, more sustainable, and far less
> vulnerable to political upheaval."

The United States Faces an Energy Crisis

Paul Roberts

*In the following viewpoint Paul Roberts asserts that due to
shrinking global oil production, the United States will soon face
an oil shortage. In his opinion this could be devastating because
the U.S. economy relies heavily on oil. In addition, Roberts
points out, while there are potential alternative sources of energy
to replace oil, these are currently expensive and plagued by technical problems. He believes that the United States is unprepared
for an impending energy crisis. Roberts' articles on oil have ap-
peared in numerous publications, including* Harper's Magazine,
the Los Angeles Times, *and* Newsweek. *He is also the author of*
The End of Oil.

As you read, consider the following questions:

1. According to the author, why does America's current
   energy infrastructure make it difficult to wean the country from fossil fuels?

2. What is the biggest problem with hydrogen as an energy
   source, according to Roberts?

Paul Roberts, "Over a Barrel," *Mother Jones*, vol. 29, November/December 2004, p. 64.

3. In the author's opinion, why is it undesirable for the
   United States to be forced to find short-term fixes in the
   case of an oil shortage?

It's eight o'clock on a fresh summer morning in Denver,
and I'm at a podium before a hundred executives from regional energy companies. Having spent the last few years
closely observing trends in the oil industry, I'm often asked to
speak about the decline of global energy supplies, the way oil
has corrupted U.S. foreign policy, and why the worldwide energy economy needs a radical transformation if we want to
avoid catastrophic climate change. Yet while these themes play
well to liberal audiences in Boulder and Berkeley, I worry, my
reception here will be much cooler. Most of these weather-
beaten men (and a few women) spend their days squeezing
hydrocarbons from the sand and stone beneath the Rockies: if
my past observations of the energy industry are any guide,
they voted for [George W.] Bush, support the Iraq war, think
climate change is a leftist hoax, and believe the main cause of
America's energy crisis is that overzealous regulation keeps
drillers like themselves from tapping the most promising reserves of oil and natural gas.

But as I finish my spiel and take questions, my initial assumptions vanish. When I suggest that the Iraq war might not
have been motivated entirely by America's thirst for oil, many
in the room openly smirk, as if I've just suggested that the
world is flat. Likewise, few here seem to share the White
House's Panglossian[1] view that the United States is sitting atop
some massive, but politically off-limits, reserve of natural gas.
In fact, as much as these executives would love to sink their
drills anywhere they want—and as much as they detest environmentalists for stopping them—no one here believes the
volume of natural gas yet to be discovered in the Rockies, or
anywhere else in America, would reverse the nation's decline

1. unfoundedly optimistic

of gas production or let the United States move to a cleaner, more secure "gas" economy. As one executive tells me, "even if all the off-limits land were opened for drilling, all the new gas we could bring on-line wouldn't be enough to replace all the production we're losing from older fields. We'd barely keep production flat."

Decreasing Oil Production

For those who wonder where the world will be getting its energy a decade from now, confessions like these only confirm what many have feared for some time: namely, that the cheap, "easy" oil and natural gas that powered industrial growth for a century no longer exist in such easy abundance; and that we may have a lot less time than we thought to replace that system with something cleaner, more sustainable, and far less vulnerable to political upheaval.

The evidence is certainly piling up. Pollution levels from cars and power plants are on the rise. Climate change, another energy-related disaster, has begun impacting crop yields and water supplies and may soon provoke political strife. In fact, according to a Pentagon report last October [2003], global warming could make key resources so scarce, and nations so desperate, that "disruption and conflict will be endemic" and "warfare would define human life."

Yet the most alarming symptoms of an energy system on the verge of collapse are found in the oil markets. Today, even as global demand for oil, led by the economic boom in Asia, is rising far faster than anticipated, our ability to pump more oil is falling. Despite assurances from oil's two biggest players—the House of Bush and the House of Saud[2] —that supplies are plentiful (and, as George W. Bush famously put it, that getting the oil is just a matter of "jaw-boning our friends in OPEC [Organization of the Petroleum Exporting Countries] to open the spigots"), it's now clear that even the Saudis

2. the royal family of Saudi Arabia

lack the physical capacity to bring enough oil to desperate consumers. As a result, oil markets are now so tight that even a minor disturbance—accelerated fighting in Iraq, another bomb in Riyadh, more unrest in Venezuela or Nigeria—could send prices soaring and crash the global economy into a recession. "The world really has run out of production capacity," a veteran oil analyst warned me in late August [2004]. "Iraq is producing less than a third of the oil that had been forecast, the Saudis are maxed out, and there is no place else to go. And America is still relying on an energy policy that hasn't changed significantly in 20 years."

Nor is it any longer a matter of simply drilling new wells or laying new pipe. Oil is finite, and eventually, global production must peak, much as happened to domestic supplies in the early 1970s. When it does, oil prices will leap, perhaps as high as $100 per barrel—a disaster if we don't have a cost-effective alternative fuel or technology in place. When the peak is coming is impossible to predict with precision. Estimates range from the ultra-optimistic, which foresee a peak no sooner than 2035, to the pessimistic, which hold that the peak may have already occurred. In any case, the signs are clear that the easy oil is harder to find and what remains is increasingly difficult and expensive to extract. Already, Western oil companies are struggling to discover new supplies fast enough to replace the oil they are selling. . . .

Worse, according to a new study in the respected *Petroleum Review*, in the United Kingdom, Indonesia, Gabon, and 15 other oil-rich nations that now supply 30 percent of the world's daily crude, oil production—that is, the number of barrels that are pumped each day—is declining by 5 percent a year. That's double the rate of decline of even a year ago, and it has forced other oil producers to pump extra simply to keep global supplies steady. "Those producers still with expansion potential are having to work harder and harder just to make up for the accelerating losses of the large number that have clearly peaked and are now in continuous decline," writes Chris Skrebowski, editor of *Petroleum Review* and a former analyst with BP [British Petroleum] and the Saudi national oil company. "Though largely unrecognized, [depletion] may be contributing to the rise in oil prices."

Signs of Awareness

If there is one positive sign, it's that the high prices seem to have finally broken through America's wall of energy denial. In fact, while energy experts like Skrebowski have been fretting about oil dependency and depleting reserves since the 1970s, today's energy anxiety is no longer coming simply from academia or the political margins. In recent months, energy problems have come under intense focus by the mainstream media, filling radio and TV talk shows and newsmagazines. Whereas official U.S. policy still blames OPEC for our oil woes, even right-of-center, pro-business outlets like *Business Week, The Economist,* and *Fortune* have acceded that the biggest risk for U.S. energy security isn't "foreign" producers or even environmentalists, but rather a decades-old domestic energy policy that remains focused almost entirely on finding new supplies while doing nothing to curb demand. "Much as we might like to, we can't blame it on OPEC," noted *Fortune,* in August [2004]. "After all, Americans have been on a two-decade oil pig-out, gorging like oversized vacationers at a Vegas buffet."

What's more, while a powerful, ideologically driven minority—led, sadly, by the Bush administration—continues to insist that energy security is simply a question of drilling in the Arctic National Wildlife Refuge (ANWR) or browbeating OPEC, outside the White House, and certainly outside the Beltway [i.e., outside the Washington, D.C., area], there's a growing push to build a fundamentally new energy system. . . . The corporate world, once a stalwart opponent of any policy reform, has become startlingly progressive. Toyota and Honda

Toles. © by Universal Press Syndicate. Reproduced by permission.

are busily rolling out hybrid cars. Agriculture and insurance firms warn of the future costs of oil-price swings and climate change. And energy companies like BP and Shell, eager to profit in the new energy order, are developing new fuels and technologies to help reduce oil use and emissions. . . .

"Killer" Flaws

Unfortunately, as encouraging as all this new energy awareness is, actually weaning the United States from fossil fuels is far easier said than done. To begin with, our current energy infrastructure—the pipelines and refineries, the power plants and grids, the gasoline stations, and, of course, the cars, trucks, planes, and ships—is a massive, sprawling asset that took more than a century to build and is worth some $1 trillion. Replacing that hydrocarbon monster with "clean" technologies and fuels before our current energy problems escalate into catastrophes will likely be the most complex and expensive challenge this country has ever faced.

And just as we've tended to underplay the flaws in our hydrocarbon energy system, we've also held far too rosy a notion of the various energy alternatives that are supposed to replace oil. In fact, to the extent that most politicians even discuss alternative energy, it tends to be in the rhetoric of American Can-Doism, a triumphant vision in which the same blend of technological prowess, entrepreneurial spirit, and market forces that helped us build an atom bomb, put a man on the moon, and produce the TV dinner and the microchip can now be counted on to yield a similar miracle in energy. Thus we find ourselves imagining a future powered by solar cells, bio-diesel, wind farms, tidal power, cold fusion, and, of course, hydrogen fuel cells, all currently being created in busy research labs and brought to us by a Free Market that is responding naturally, efficiently, and inexorably to the rising price of oil.

Yet the hard truth is that this hyper-optimistic dream is plagued by a variety of potentially killer flaws. First, many of these new technologies are nowhere near ready for prime time, and exist mainly in the conceptual stage, if that. Second, of the alternative fuels and gadgets that are technically viable today, many simply cannot compete with fossil fuels or existing technologies. Third, while the market is indeed a marvelous mechanism for bringing innovation to life, the modern economy doesn't even recognize that the current energy system needs replacing. You and I may know that hydrocarbons cost us dearly, in terms of smog, climate change, corruption, and instability, not to mention the billions spent defending the Middle East. But because these "external" costs aren't included in the price of a gallon of gasoline, the market sees no reason to find something other than oil, gas, or coal.

New Technologies Plagued with Problems

In late July 2004, financial analysts from across North America joined a conference call with Dennis Campbell, the embattled president of a shrinking Canadian company called Ballard Power Systems. Just a few years before, Ballard had been the toast of energy investors and the acknowledged leader in the campaign to move beyond oil. Its main product, a compact hydrogen fuel cell that could power a car, was widely hailed as the breakthrough that would smash the century-long reign of the gasoline-powered internal combustion engine. In early 2000, Ballard shares were trading for $120, allowing the company to raise a near-record $340.7 million in financing and touching off a wave of expectations that a fuel-cell revolution was imminent.

Since then, however, as fuel cells have been hobbled by technical problems, Ballard has seen its share value plummet to $8, as energy investors have all but abandoned hydrogen in favor of the latest energy darling, the gas-electric hybrid. During the conference call, Campbell insisted that hybrids were only a temporary fix, and that fuel cells remained the only long-term solution to problems like climate change and declining energy supplies. He was, however, forced to acknowledge that consumers and businesses alike were "discouraged by the long wait and the uncertain timelines" for fuel cells and had been "seduced by the lure of an easier solution to the energy and environmental challenges that we face."

In many respects, Ballard is the perfect cautionary tale for the entire roster of alternative fuels and energy technologies, which, for all their huge promise, are, upon closer inspection, plagued by problems. For example, many energy experts see natural gas as the most logical interim step in eventually weaning ourselves from oil. Natural gas emits less carbon dioxide and pollutants than does oil (and certainly coal); it can be used in everything from cars to power plants; it's also easily refined into hydrogen—all of which make it the perfect "bridge" fuel between the current oil-based economy and something new. But even as demand for gas grows in the United States, domestic production is in decline, meaning we'll have to import an increasing volume via pipelines from

Canada or through liquefied natural gas terminals in port cities. Even assuming we overcome the political hurdles, simply building this costly new infrastructure will take years, and, once completed, will leave us dependent on many of the same countries that now control the oil business. (The biggest gas reserves are in the Middle East and Russia.) . . .

Solar and Wind Power

And what about solar and wind? As it turns out, the two most famous alternative energy technologies together generate less than half a percent of the planet's energy. Here's a depressing fact: The entire output of every solar photovoltaic (PV) cell currently installed worldwide—about 2,000 megawatts total—is less than the output of just two conventional, coal-fired power plants.

Why do alternatives own such a puny share of the market? According to conventional wisdom, Big Oil and Big Coal use their massive economic power to corrupt Big Government, which then hands out massive subsidies and tax breaks for oil and coal, giving hydrocarbons an unbeatable advantage over alternatives. In truth, much of the fault lies with the new energy technologies themselves, which simply cannot yet compete effectively with fossil fuels.

Consider the saga of the solar cell. Despite decades of research and development, solar power still costs more than electricity generated from a gas- or coal-fired power plant. And although PV cell costs will continue to fall, there remains the problem of "intermittency"—solar only works when the sun is shining, whereas a conventional power plant can crank out power 24 hours a day, 365 days a year. (Wind presents a similar problem.) To use solar and wind, utilities must have backup power, probably coal- or gas-fired plants. . . .

Hydrogen Power

The most dramatic example of the mismatch between fossil fuels and their would-be competitors, however, can be found in the fuel cell. For decades, hydrogen proponents have argued that fuel cells, which turn hydrogen and oxygen into electricity while emitting only water vapor, are the key to the next energy economy. Like a battery that never needs charging, fuel cells can power office buildings, laptops, and especially cars, where they are roughly three times as efficient as a traditional internal combustion engine. And because you can make hydrogen by running electric current through water, advocates envisioned a global system in which power from solar, wind, and other renewables would be turned into hydrogen.

This compelling vision helps explain why the "hydrogen economy" was so touted during the 1990s, and why companies like Ballard Power Systems could partner with giants like Daimler-Chrysler and Ford, igniting a fuel-cell mania that dazzled investors and policymakers alike. Indeed, in his 2003 State of the Union address, President Bush vowed that, within 20 years, fuel cells would "make our air significantly cleaner, and our country much less dependent on foreign sources of oil."

In truth, even as the president was promising better living through hydrogen, the reality of a hydrogen economy was moving farther and farther away. While the basic technology remains promising, making hydrogen turns out to be far more difficult than advertised. The easiest and by far cheapest method—splitting natural gas into carbon and hydrogen—is hampered by domestic shortages of natural gas. And while it is possible to extract hydrogen from water using renewably generated electricity, that concept suffers from the power-density problem. Studies by Jim MacKenzie, a veteran energy analyst with the World Resources Institute, show that a solar-powered hydrogen economy in the United States would require at least 160,000 square miles of photovoltaic panels—an area slightly larger than the state of California—and would increase national water consumption by 10 percent. "We could do it," MacKenzie told me last year. "But it would be expensive."

But hydrogen's biggest problem is the fuel cell itself, which, despite decades of research, is still too expensive and unreliable to compete with the internal combustion engine. As of last year [2003], the best fuel cells were still 10 times as costly as an equivalently powered gasoline engine. Hydrogen advocates argue that once fuel cells can be mass-produced, costs will drop dramatically. Yet while that's true, it's also true that gasoline engines will also improve over time—in fact, they already have. With the gasoline-electric hybrid, for example, the internal combustion engine has, in a stroke, doubled its fuel economy and halved its emissions—but without forcing consumers to use a complicated new technology or fuel. Barring some technological breakthrough that dramatically lowers costs or improves performance, the fuel cell may remain one step behind the gasoline engine for a long time, further delaying the moment it can begin displacing its hydrocarbon rival. . . .

A Dangerous Position

A true energy revolution—one that begins moving away from fossil fuels entirely—can't succeed or even get started until we can somehow induce the market to "see" the true costs of energy, and, specifically, just how environmentally and politically expensive "cheap" fossil fuels really are. . . .

Supply and demand are today so tightly balanced that even the smallest incident in an oil-producing country could send prices into the stratosphere, destroying economies and forcing big, oil-dependent nations like the United States and China to opt for emergency short-term fixes—fixes that aren't likely to involve methodical programs to improve automotive efficiency or develop cost-effective ethanol. Rather, once the United States finds itself in a real energy emergency, it will do what desperate states have always done when resources turn scarce: fight for them. In other words, the most pressing question may not be whether we have the right technologies, but whether we have enough time.

After the peak, comes the fall.

When conventional oil production peaks ... nations will increasingly turn to much more difficult-to-extract sources, such as reserves found under the Arctic ice caps or far out to sea, heavy oil distilled from sand tar, or natural gas liquids such as butane. But eventually, these sources, too, will peter out.

> "The current, robust demand for energy will lead to a new age of energy innovation and abundance."

The United States Does Not Face an Energy Crisis

Dennis Behreandt

America has an abundance of possible energy sources, maintains Dennis Behreandt in the following viewpoint, and will not face an energy crisis caused by reduced oil supplies. In Behreandt's opinion there are extensive remaining reserves of oil. In addition, he argues, history shows that as oil becomes more expensive to extract, society will transition to new energy sources. He believes that market demand for energy will spur numerous affordable alternatives to oil, such as fuel cells and nuclear power. Behreandt is a contributing writer for the New American, a biweekly, conservative magazine that offers analysis of current events.

As you read, consider the following questions:

1. According to the author, what energy source facilitated the industrial revolution?
2. As cited by Behreandt, what is the size of America's coal reserves?
3. Why has nuclear power in the United States been brought to a virtual standstill, in the author's opinion?

Dennis Behreandt, "Energy's Future," *New American*, vol. 21, April 4, 2005, pp. 10–16.
Copyright © 2005 by American Opinion Publishing Inc. Reproduced by permission.

It's hard to escape the conclusion that America faces a new, and perhaps serious, energy crisis. Home heating costs have risen dramatically, the price of gasoline at the pump is rising rapidly, and the price of crude oil is on the increase. The rising cost of fuel will affect consumers of all goods, as the cost of bringing those goods to market will rise in concert with the rise in the cost of fuel.

At least for now, there does not appear to be any relief in sight, as demand for oil is expected to continue to grow. On March 11 [2005] the Paris-based International Energy Agency (IEA) announced its latest forecast for energy demand. The agency expects that global consumption of oil will climb this year to 84.3 million barrels per day, a 2.2 percent increase over the previous year.

Importantly, the world is not running out of oil. The current crisis stems not from the depletion of the Earth's oil resources, but from the inability of current infrastructure to support the increased demand. "The reality is that oil consumption has caught up with installed crude and refining capacity," the IEA said. "If supply continues to struggle to keep up, more policy attention may come to be directed at oil demand intensity in our economies and alternatives."

The IEA is partially correct: more effort is needed to develop energy technologies, whether that effort is within the fossil fuels industry or in advancements in alternative technologies. The answer, though, does not lie with "more policy attention" directed by governments at influencing market trends. In fact, government regulations are directly responsible for limiting our refinery capacity.

If left alone, the market demand for energy will spur competition to invest in new infrastructure and new technologies. The current energy environment, marked by strong demand, will result in increased spending on exploration for new energy sources and on new energy technologies. Similar "crises" in the past were alleviated through just this type of investment and innovation. If left unhampered by government, there is no telling what energy technologies will be achieved in the near future by innovators eager to supply the world's increasing appetite for energy.

Tales of Shortages Past

In many ways, the current energy environment bears similarities with an era that seems far removed from our current technological age. In the late Renaissance and early modern period, Europe underwent a technological revolution in energy and productivity. . . .

Prior to this period, the primary motive energy source in Europe was muscle power, either human or animal. For heating and cooking, wood played a primary role. Later, following the Renaissance, Europe's commercial success continued to expand, and with it population expanded. Growth was sustained by energy. At sea, naval technology was increasingly able to harness the power of the wind, allowing European nations to engage in ever more vigorous trade with distant lands.

Within Europe itself, forests provided plenty of wood for domestic energy needs. But demand eventually began to outstrip the ability of the existing infrastructure to bring energy to market, and costs rose. "The agrarian regime . . . encountered inherent limits that it could not transcend without a fundamental transformation of its social metabolic basis," wrote German historian Rolf Peter Sieferle about energy availability in the 1700s. "These observations speak for the fact that in the 18th century the preindustrial . . . system stood at a threshold impeding the growth of important physical parameters (population size, material flow). The energy potential of the given area was in a sense exhausted."

The preindustrial energy system was heavily dependent on wood. The rising demand for wood reduced the supply, causing prices to rise. "Pundits rang the alarm bells about the soaring cost of wood for heating and for the iron industry;

the price of charcoal [made from wood] doubled in real terms between 1630 and 1700," writes business journalist Vijay V. Vaitheeswaran in his recent book *Power to the People*. The rise in prices spurred by the increased demand for energy led to the development of new and previously little-used energy sources. "Enticed by rising prices, entrepreneurs rose to the occasion," wrote Vaitheeswaran. "They found a way to bring to market a substance that had largely been overlooked until then: coal. That was a turning point in history, for without coal there would have been no industrial revolution."

The Rise of Industry

The industrial revolution may have seen the rise of all manner of innovation, but it was without doubt built on the back of King Coal, which replaced wood as the most dominant energy source. "Day by day it becomes more evident that the coal we happily possess in excellent quality and abundance is the mainspring of modern material civilization," British economist William Stanley Jevons wrote in his book *The Coal Question*, published in 1865. "As the source of fire, it is the source at once of mechanical motion and of chemical change. Accordingly it is the chief agent in almost every improvement or discovery in the arts which the present age brings forth."

However, Jevons did not think that the rapid increase in coal production to support the "present age" was sustainable. He opined that England's rapacious appetite for energy would soon consume the nation's coal reserves. "I draw the conclusion that I think anyone would draw, that *we cannot long maintain our present rate of increase of consumption; that we can never advance to the higher amounts of consumption supposed.*" In the end, Jevons thought, England would run out of coal by 1900.

Jevons needn't have worried. As before, demand for energy made innovation worthwhile, and another form of fuel was brought to market. It was time to turn to crude oil.

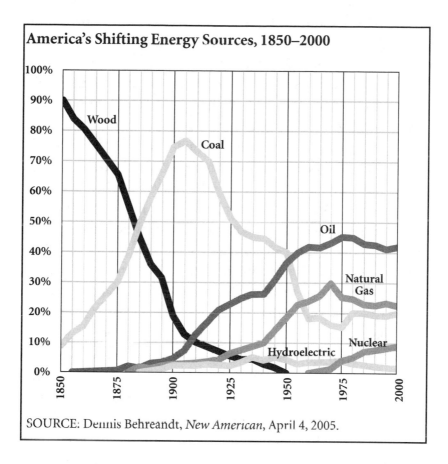

America's Shifting Energy Sources, 1850–2000

SOURCE: Dennis Behreandt, *New American*, April 4, 2005.

Oil

This fuel had been known for centuries. The Romans burned it as a fumigant. In Borneo, it had been used for heat and light. But as the 20th century drew near, this fuel would become the lifeblood of the world's economy. Early wells were shallow, limited by insufficient drill technology. All that changed on January 10, 1901. Two brothers, Al and Curt Hammil, using a new rotary drill technology, bored through more than 1,000 feet of Texas soil on a small hill called Spindletop. Just when it seemed as if they should give up, the drill punctured a pressurized dome of fossil fuel. Methane gas came howling from the drill with a roar, followed by a geyser of oil.

There was more oil than anyone had ever imagined. Most wells of the day were shallow and produced from 50 to 100 barrels per day. Spindletop produced 100,000 barrels per day. A confluence of events was now occurring that would make oil the most important fuel in the world. The internal combustion engine would shortly be combined with a horseless carriage, and diesel and gasoline refined from crude oil would power the new transportation device. Coal had been used to power steam engines, but oil quickly became the fuel of choice for those too. "As oil prices fell, coal users began switching in droves to the more efficient oil," author Paul Roberts wrote in his recent book, *The End of Oil*. "Railroads converted their coal-fired locomotives to burn cheap Texas crude. Shipping companies, quickly recognizing that oil made their ships go faster—and also that it took up less storage room onboard than coal did—refitted cargo vessels to run on oil."

Since Spindletop, oil has been king. And, for a good part of the 20th century, the United States was both the top producer and consumer of oil. By 1946, however, the nation was actually consuming more oil than it produced, a condition that has persisted to the present. Since then, there has been an ever-present chorus of those claiming that the world is about to run out of oil.

"Ever since oil was first harvested in the 1800s, people have said we'd run out of the stuff," noted John Felmy, the chief economist at the American Petroleum Institute. These predictions have come to naught, says science journalist Kevin Kelleher. "In the 1880s a Standard Oil executive sold off shares in the company out of fear that its reserves were close to drying up," Kelleher wrote in the August 2004 issue of *Popular Science*. Similarly, in 1977, President Jimmy Carter warned that mankind "could use up all the proven reserves of oil in the entire world by the end of the next decade." That wasn't true then, and it isn't true now.

It is, of course, true that there is more demand for oil today from other quarters of the world than there was previously. Whereas North America and Europe had been far and away the major consumers of energy throughout most of the last century, now emerging industrialized economies in Asia, notably China, are competing for the resource. And yet, the world is not running out of oil. There is, in fact, quite a large amount of oil remaining.

In the U.S. alone in 2003, according to the U.S. Energy Information Agency [EIA], proved reserves (meaning oil that can be recovered from existing reservoirs under current operational and economic conditions) totaled some 21.8 billion barrels. Worldwide, in 2003 proved reserves totaled 1.15 trillion barrels, enough to last for 41 years, according to the giant oil firm British Petroleum (BP). "Despite those who say we are about to run out of oil and gas, the figures in the review confirm there is no shortage of reserves," said BP chief economist Peter Davies.

At the current rate of consumption, it appears that the world's proved reserves will be consumed in approximately 30 or 40 years. This, however, may not be likely. Proved reserves are only those reserves that are feasibly recoverable, both economically and technologically, at a given time. As technology improves and demand increases, it will become practical to recover more oil, increasing proved reserves. . . .

It is worth considering, in addition, that many domestic resources have been placed off-limits by government regulation. In fact, according to the EIA, 78.6 percent of technically recoverable resources are located on federal land. The Arctic National Wildlife Refuge (ANWR) is a case in point. The ANWR sits upon vast amounts of recoverable oil on a par with the current largest U.S. oil field at Prudhoe Bay. The oil could be recovered with negligible impact to the environment of the area, yet opening the ANWR to drilling continues to be resisted.

Similarly, much of the outer continental shelf off the nation's coasts has been made off-limits, despite the very real possibility that important energy resources may be located there. In addition, other deposits of oil and other substances in the contiguous states have been made off-limits by virtue of the fact that they are located on federal land. The energy future, in fact, would be very bright if government would simply get out of the way and allow entrepreneurs to develop our known energy resources and discover new ones. . . .

Old Fuels and New Tricks

Even though technology will make it possible to continue to supply the world's oil needs, the increased demand for energy may make other fuels attractive. The United States sits atop an almost unimaginably vast store of relatively high quality coal. As an energy source, coal is supposed to be passé. Widely regarded as a dirty substance that kills miners and pollutes the air with choking soot and poisonous sulphur dioxide, it was supposed to have been relegated to the dustbin of history by cleaner burning oil and natural gas.

That coal is still vital is illustrated by the career of Corbin Robertson, Jr. Robertson's family turned oil into a billion dollar business with Quintana Petroleum. But the young Corbin gave it all up for coal. "I bet the ranch and all the cows on it," Robertson told *Forbes* magazine in 2003. "I even hocked the Tom O'Conner [oil] Field."

In part, the attraction of coal is its sheer quantity. According to the National Mining Association, in 2003 U.S. coal reserves stood at a staggering 496 billion tons. At present rates of consumption, these reserves will supply U.S. coal needs for more than 200 years. Coal is presently, and will continue to be, important to the U.S. energy supply. According to the Energy Information Agency, "Coal is projected to fuel roughly 50% of electricity generation through 2025." Even so, coal prices are expected to hold steady or even decline over the same period, making it an ever more attractive fuel option.

Innovation may make coal even more essential. Coal can be turned into a gas. Many years ago, this gas was used to provide fuel for gaslights. But now some generating stations are being built that use the gas to generate electricity. Integrated Gasification Combined Cycle (IGCC) power plants first turn coal into gas, then use the gas to power gas-fired turbines, making electricity. In the process, they produce CO_2 that could be used in efforts to recover oil from "depleted" wells. Moreover, the process of gasification produces hydrogen, itself an energy source with vast potential for the future. . . .

Of Fuel Cells and Fission

Fuel cell–powered cars may prove to be the most important technological innovation since the internal combustion engine. Currently, much of the oil recovered from the world's oil fields is refined into the fuels used by the internal combustion engines powering the world's fleet of cars and trucks. Naturally, the demand for oil for this purpose would be significantly diminished if fuel cell–powered vehicles live up to their promise. There are, however, difficulties to be overcome.

Fuel cells are deceptively simple. They work by combining hydrogen with oxygen to create water, producing electricity in the process. The only byproduct is water. Because the process is silent and results in electricity, automobile designers are presented with design possibilities never before attainable due to constraints imposed by the internal combustion engine and the gearing mechanisms needed to harness its power. Suddenly, completely silent automobiles featuring "fly-by-wire" controls become feasible.

The chief problem with fuel cells is the fuel. Hydrogen is difficult to store and not easily accessible at present. Though hydrogen is the most abundant element in the universe, it is almost invariably found in combination with other elements and must be freed for use. This itself takes energy. Fortunately, this can be overcome by coal-fired IGCC power plants. Still, the infrastructure needed to store and distribute the hydrogen will be needed. Another option will be to power fuel cells with more complex hydrocarbons, like methane, and reform them "onboard" for use in the fuel cell. This less efficient method may be an intermediate solution.

So are fuel cells just some futurist's pipe dream? Based on the fact that they are being employed commercially, the answer must be "no." General Motors [GM] for instance, has entered into a deal with Dow Chemical to provide fuel cell technology to power a Dow plant. According to a GM overview of the plan, "The initial GM fuel cell will generate 75 kilowatts of power. This is enough electricity for fifty average homes. Dow and GM plan to ultimately install up to 400 fuel cells to generate 35 megawatts of electricity. That would be enough power for 25,000 average sized American homes."

Fuel cells aren't the only futuristic energy technology that will probably play a significant role in the near future. Another is a technology that has already been producing power for nearly 50 years but still seems futuristic nonetheless: nuclear energy. Prior to the nuclear age, splitting the atom was considered an impossibility. Albert Einstein, the famous physicist, argued, "There is not the slightest indication that [nuclear] energy will ever be obtainable. It would mean that the atom would have to be shattered at will." Work completed by [physicist] Enrico Fermi and others, though, caused Einstein to change his mind.

Nuclear power, an American innovation, has been brought to a virtual standstill in this country, because of political, not technological, obstacles. Yet it is still a viable and important energy source. According to the federal Energy Information Agency [EIA], U.S. nuclear facilities had a record year in 2004. The EIA reported: "The U.S. nuclear industry generated 788,556 million kilowatt hours of electricity in 2004, a new

U.S. (and international) record. Although no new U.S. nuclear power plants have come online since 1996, this is the industry's fifth annual record since 1998." There are currently 104 licensed nuclear power generating stations operating within the United States. The energy they produce accounts for about 20 percent of the nation's electricity and about 8 percent of the total energy we consume.

These figures could be higher, as evidenced by the fact that many other nations, taking full advantage of the technology the United States developed, are using nuclear technology to produce a much higher percentage of their electricity from nuclear power than we are. . . .

The Future Is Bright

The future is not limited to the fossil fuels and nuclear fission of the past century. Just as the last 100 years have witnessed almost unimaginable advances in technology, the next 100 years will almost certainly be just as revolutionary. "[O]ver the next few decades, we are very likely to see all kinds of technological advances that have nothing to do with hydrocarbons, or solar, or wind, for that matter—advances that most of us, brought up in the age of oil, probably can't even imagine," writes journalist Paul Roberts in his book, The End of Oil. . . .

Still, there's no telling what these advances and others yet unimagined may bring. One thing is certain, though. The current energy crisis marked by the rapidly rising cost of petroleum will be like other such crises in the past. It will not be an indication that a resource is being depleted, because, like wood and coal of earlier days, oil continues to exist in abundance. The rising cost does mean, though, that vast opportunities exist for innovators and investors who seek to bring new technologies to market. The risks are high, but the rewards are great. If the past is a guide, the current, robust demand for energy will lead to a new age of energy innovation and abundance.

> "Saudi Arabia is about to face exhaus-
> tion of its giant fields and will prob-
> ably experience a sharp decline in out-
> put relatively soon."

The Depletion of Saudi Arabian Oil Supplies Will Cause an Oil Crisis

Michael T. Klare

In the following viewpoint Michael T. Klare discusses Saudi Arabia's oil supplies in light of recent research on the subject by energy investment broker Matthew Simmons. Saudi Arabia's oil is vital to meeting world demand, explains Klare, yet according to Simmons, Saudi Arabia will soon experience a sharp decline in output. Klare believes this will lead to a worldwide oil shortage. He warns that in order to prevent a crisis, steps must be taken now to limit oil consumption and develop energy alternatives. Klare is a professor and director of the Five College Program in Peace and World Security Studies at Hampshire College, Massachusetts, and author of Blood and Oil: The Dangers of America's Growing Petroleum Dependency.

As you read, consider the following questions:

1. According to the U.S. Department of Energy, as cited by Klare, how much of the world's proven oil reserves are located in Saudi Arabia?

Michael T. Klare, "The Vanishing Mirage of Saudi Oil," *Los Angeles Times*, June 27, 2005, p. B9. Copyright © 2005 by Michael T. Klare. Reproduced by permission.

2. Where does most of Saudi Arabia's oil come from, according to the author?

3. As explained by Klare, why will an oil shortage cause the cost of food to rise?

For those oil enthusiasts who believe that petroleum will remain abundant for decades to come—among them, the president, vice president and their many friends in the oil industry—any talk of an imminent "peak" in global oil production and an ensuing decline can be easily countered with a simple mantra: "Saudi Arabia, Saudi Arabia, Saudi Arabia."

Not only will the Saudis pump extra oil now to alleviate global shortages, as is claimed, but they will keep pumping more in the years ahead to quench our insatiable thirst for energy. And when the kingdom's existing fields run dry, lo, they will begin pumping from other fields that are just waiting to be exploited. This is the basis for the administration's contention that we can continue to increase our yearly consumption of oil, rather than conserve what's left and begin the transition to a post-petroleum economy.

Doubts About Saudi Oil

But that may not be the case. In a newly released book, investment banker Matthew R. Simmons convincingly demonstrates that, far from being capable of increasing its output, Saudi Arabia is about to face exhaustion of its giant fields and will probably experience a sharp decline in output relatively soon. He also argues that there is little chance that Saudi Arabia will ever discover new fields that can take up the slack from those now in decline.

If Simmons is right about Saudi Arabian oil production—and the official dogma is wrong—we can kiss the era of abundant petroleum goodbye forever. This is so for a simple reason: Saudi Arabia is the world's leading oil producer, and there is no other major supplier (or combination of suppliers) capable of making up for the loss in Saudi production if its output falters.

The Importance of Saudi Oil

According to the U.S. Department of Energy [DOE] Saudi Arabia possesses about one-fourth of the world's proven oil reserves, an estimated 264 billion barrels. Also, the Saudis are believed to harbor additional reserves containing another few hundred-billion barrels. On this basis, the department asserts that "Saudi Arabia is likely to remain the world's largest oil producer for the foreseeable future."

Consider the DOE's projections. Because of the rapidly growing international thirst for petroleum—much of it coming from the United States and Europe, but an increasing share from China, India and other developing nations—the world's expected requirement for petroleum is projected to jump from 77 million barrels per day in 2001 to 121 million barrels by 2025. Fortunately, says the DOE, global oil output will also rise by this amount in the years ahead. But over one-fourth of this additional oil—about 12.3 million barrels per day—will have to come from Saudi Arabia.

The problem is, if you take away Saudi Arabia's 12.3 million barrels, there is no possibility of satisfying anticipated world demand in 2025.

The Saudis vehemently deny their fields are in decline. The DOE, with no independent verification, backs them up. In the end, it comes down to this: America's entire energy strategy, with its commitment to an increased reliance on petroleum as the major source of our energy, rests on the unproven claims of Saudi oil producers that they can continuously increase Saudi output in accordance with the DOE predictions.

Interview with Matthew Simmons

Lise Doucette: Matthew Simmons is Chairman and CEO of Simmons and Company International; it's a Houston-based investment bank specializing in the energy sector. His new book, Twilight in the Desert: The Coming Saudi Oil Shock and the World Economy, *is, he says, meant to scare us to death. So on this morning he joins us from Portland, Maine. Good Morning.*

Matthew Simmons: Good morning. How are you?

Good morning. Yes, fine thank you, well at least until I hear what you have to tell to us. Now, the new leader of Saudi Arabia, Crown Prince Abdullah, says that they will continue their long standing oil policy which is to keep the markets well supplied. Do you believe that's possible to keep?

I believe that they believe that it's possible, and that's probably one of the things that worries me the most. I think they're relying on the fact that for seventy years they've been able to keep this miracle going with a small number of fields, and my worry, based on two years of research through technical papers all written by technicians working within the national oil company in Saudi Arabia, would indicate that there's a real risk that their current rate of production can't be sustained for much longer and that the longer they produce at these rates, let alone increase the rates, they're risking production collapse in all of their key fields.

Global Public Media, "Saudi Oil Shortage," August 3, 2005. www.globalpublicmedia.com.

Simmons' Argument

And this is where Simmons enters the picture, with his meticulously documented book, "Twilight in the Desert." Simmons is not a militant environmentalist or anti-oil partisan; he is chairman and CEO of one of the nation's leading oil-industry investment banks, Simmons & Co. International. For decades, he has been financing the exploration and development of new oil reservoirs. In the process, he has become a friend and associate of many of the top figures in the oil industry, including George W. Bush and [U.S. vice president] Dick Cheney.

Essentially, Simmons' argument boils down to four major points:

1. Most of Saudi Arabia's oil output is generated by a few giant fields, of which Ghawar—the world's largest—is the most prolific.
2. These giant fields were first developed 40 to 50 years ago, and have since given up much of their easily extracted petroleum.
3. To maintain high levels of production in these major fields, the Saudis have come to rely increasingly on the use of water injection and other secondary recovery methods to compensate for the drop in natural field pressure.
4. As time passes, the ratio of water to oil in these underground fields rises to the point where further oil extraction becomes difficult, if not impossible. To top it all off, there is very little reason to assume that future Saudi exploration will result in the discovery of new fields to replace those now in decline.

This being the case, Simmons concludes, it would be the height of folly to assume that the Saudis are capable of doubling their petroleum output in the years ahead, as projected by the DOE.

Time to Act

The moment that Saudi production goes into permanent decline in the not-too-distant future, the Petroleum Age as we know it will draw to a close. Oil will still be available on international markets, but not in the abundance to which we have become accustomed and not at a price that many of us will be able to afford. Transportation, and everything it affects—virtually the entire world economy—will be much more costly. The cost of food will also rise, as modern agriculture relies to an extraordinary extent on petroleum products for tilling, harvesting, protecting, processing and delivery. Many other products made with petroleum—paints, plastics, lubricants, pharmaceuticals, cosmetics and so forth—will also prove far more costly. Under these circumstances, a global economic contraction appears nearly inevitable.

Only if we act now to limit our consumption of oil and develop non-petroleum energy alternatives, can we face the "twilight" of the Petroleum Age with some degree of hope; if we fail to do so, we are in for a very grim time.

Given the high stakes involved, there is no doubt that intense efforts will be made to refute Simmons' findings. With his book, however, it will no longer be possible for oil aficionados simply to chant "Saudi Arabia, Saudi Arabia, Saudi Arabia" and convince us that everything is all right in the oil world.

> "It is Russia that will lift the globe out
> of its current energy funk."

Oil Production by Russia Will Prevent an Oil Crisis

James Flanigan

Saudi Arabian oil is not the key to meeting rising world demand, maintains James Flanigan in the following viewpoint. Instead, he argues, Russia and other countries will meet that demand. Indeed, he claims, Russia has vast oil reserves and is steadily increasing production. While the world will eventually need to find alternative energy sources, says Flanigan, as a result of supplies from Russia and other nations, oil will not run out in the near future. Flanigan has been a writer and business columnist for the Los Angeles Times *and* New York Times *since 1983. Prior to that he spent seventeen years with* Forbes *magazine.*

As you read, consider the following questions:

1. According to the author, by how much has Russia's oil production increased in the last five years?
2. How much oil does the Athabasca oil sands in Canada hold, according to Flanigan?
3. As argued by the author, until what year will petroleum supplies be relatively abundant?

With sky-high gasoline prices burning into family budgets, the oil-using world listened anxiously last week [May 2004] for words of deliverance from the Saudi Arabian oil minister, Ali Ibrahim Naimi [who stated that Saudi Arabia would increase its oil production]. Folks would have been wiser to listen to Russian President Vladimir V. Putin.

The Importance of Russia

For as significant as Saudi production is—and as helpful as Naimi's pledge to increase petroleum output by 11% to 9 million barrels a day should be—it is Russia that will lift the globe out of its current energy funk.

In the last five years, Russia's oil production has soared 48%, thanks to steadily rising flows from new wells. The country is already producing 9 million barrels of oil a day, making it the world's largest producer.

But it isn't about to stop there. Putin and his oil ministers plan to crank up output to 11 million barrels a day in the next five years. That rise, coupled with the efforts of several other suppliers, is why crude prices— now [in May 2004] at a lofty $40 a barrel and in some eyes headed to a stratospheric $50—will settle back down to $25 by 2006.

It may sound crazy as American motorists head into the summer driving season confronted by record pump prices. But by 2010, even as developing countries such as China and India exhibit a nearly insatiable demand for energy, production from non-OPEC [Organization of the Petroleum Exporting Countries] nations probably will generate a surfeit of oil. Today's headlines—and hand-wringing—will be a distant memory.

Joseph Stanislaw, president of Cambridge Energy Research Associates, is among those who see an oil surplus ahead. He predicts that global production, now at 82 million barrels a day, will grow by 20 million barrels by decade's end.

"Key to this balance is Russia," says Stanislaw, who has just issued a report titled "Oil: How High Can It Go, and for How Long?"

New Fields in Russia

New fields in Siberia are being developed by companies that suddenly stand among the biggest anywhere. Lukoil Oil Co., Russia's largest petroleum firm, for example, is now the world's second-largest private holder of oil reserves, after Exxon Mobil Corp. (Lukoil also has acquired more than 2,000 gas stations in the U.S.)

Yukos Oil Co. and Sibneft, Russia's second- and third-ranked producers, respectively, are also developing projects in Siberia's forbidding vastness.

Russia sets aside opportunities in Siberia for homegrown companies, but it takes in partners elsewhere in its enormous territory. ConocoPhillips, for example, is in a joint venture in the Russian Arctic with Rosneft ("neft" is the Russian word for oil). And Exxon Mobil is part of a project on Sakhalin Island in the Russian Far East.

As is always the case with finding and tapping oil, collecting the prize isn't easy. For all its ambitions, Russia faces a paucity of pipeline capacity as it tries to get the stuff out of Siberia to waiting markets in Europe and Asia. Putin, in fact, stepped in personally last week to reprimand Transneft, the state-controlled firm with a monopoly on pipelines, for bureaucratic dawdling.

He made specific suggestions for pipelines that would run from eastern Siberia to the Black Sea. Putin also is pushing Yukos to pump 1 million barrels a day from its new Siberian field, even though he put Yukos' chairman, Mikhail Khodorkovsky, in jail in December.

"The government must base its decisions on the interests of the state as a whole and not on those of individual compa-

Russia's Oil Production

According to the *Oil and Gas Journal*, Russia has proven oil reserves of 60 billion barrels, most of which are located in Western Siberia, between the Ural Mountains and the Central Siberian Plateau. Approximately 14 billion barrels exist on Sakhalin Island in the far eastern region of the country, just north of Japan. . . .

A turnaround in Russian oil output, which many analysts have attributed to the privatization of the industry following the collapse of the Soviet Union, began in 1999. The privatization clarified incentives and increased less expensive production. Higher world oil prices . . . the usage of technology that was standard practice in the West, and the rejuvenation of old oil fields also helped raise production levels. . . .

Accordingly, in 2003, Russia was the world's second largest producer of crude oil, behind only Saudi Arabia. From March to May 2004, Russian crude oil output actually exceeded that of Saudi Arabia. Both the Russian government and outside observers agree that production should continue to grow, at least in the short term.

U.S. Energy Information Administration, 2005.
www.eia.doe.gov.

nies," the former KGB [Committee for State Security in the former Soviet Union] member said in a speech Wednesday.

Oil from Other Countries

Russia is not alone in adding to the world's supply of oil. Other countries, including Mexico, Nigeria and Libya came forward last week with vows to expand their output as well.

For its part, Canada plans to raise its production by 78% (to about 5 million barrels a day) this decade, mainly by increasing output from the Athabasca oil sands in northern Alberta. The sands are gigantic formations that hold more than 1.6 trillion barrels of oil—more than all the world's present reserves.

Companies don't actually drill the oil sands. Instead, they mine the muck and manufacture crude oil from a mixture of sand, water and bitumen—asphalt in its natural state.

Facilities to separate oil from the mix are expensive to build. But SunCor Energy Inc., a Calgary, Canada–based firm that controls leases on sands containing 10 billion barrels of oil, is spending $7 billion over the next five years to double its output to 500,000 barrels a day. Syncrude Canada Ltd., a consortium in which Exxon Mobil has a stake, is looking to invest a similar amount.

Of course, none of this should be taken as a signal to buy a second Hummer and trip along blithely. Petroleum remains a finite resource. Eventually, it will run out.

SunCor President Rick George notes that the use of oil energy will grow more in the next 25 years than it has in the last quarter-century. Car culture is just coming to China. The pressures on the resource base, on the capital markets to fund the development of more oil and on the environment to tolerate the burning of more hydrocarbons will expand geometrically.

What this means, in short, is that the clock is ticking.

No Imminent Crisis

This column has called attention many times to the need for our economy to diversify away from oil and gas energy. Such warnings do not mean that oil is running out today or tomorrow or even the day after that. The U.S. Geological Survey postulates that petroleum supplies will be relatively abundant until the 2040s. That gives us about 35 years to adapt.

Meanwhile, because of Russia and others, $2.50-a-gallon gasoline prices won't be the permanent fate of the car-buying public. Not yet anyway.

Periodical Bibliography

The following articles have been selected to supplement the diverse views presented in this chapter.

Tim Appenzeller	"The End of Cheap Oil," *National Geographic*, June 2004.
John Attarian	"Oil Depletion: Why the Peak Is Probably Near," *Social Contract*, Winter 2004/2005.
Robert Fri et al.	"Future Oil Supplies," *Issues in Science and Technology*, Summer 2005.
Michael T. Klare	"No Escape from Foreign Oil Dependency," *Human Quest*, January/February 2005.
Marianne Lavelle	"Living Without Oil," *U.S. News & World Report*, February 17, 2003.
Amory B. Lovins	"How to Live Without Oil," *Newsweek*, August 8, 2005.
Alan Nogee	"Fossil Fuels: Running Out of Gas," *Liberal Opinion Week*, October 11, 2004.
Peter Odell	"Oil Is Still King," *New Scientist*, November 6, 2004.
Jordan E. Powell	"After the Oil Runs Out," *Liberal Opinion Week*, June 21, 2004.
Paul Roberts	"Running Out of Oil—and Time," *Los Angeles Times*, April 29, 2004.
Matthew R. Simmons, interviewed by Jim Motavalli	"A Diminished Future for Saudi Oil," *E Magazine*, 2004. www.emagazine.com.
Jyoti Thottam	"Why Gas Won't Get Cheaper: The President's Energy Plan Won't Stop the Pain at the Pump. But There's No Reason to Panic. Here's Why," *Time*, May 9, 2005.
David Yergin	"Imagining a $7-a-Gallon Future," *New York Times*, April 4, 2004.

How Can America Reduce Domestic Oil Prices?

Chapter Preface

In October 1973 Arab members of the Organization of the Petroleum Exporting Countries (OPEC) imposed an oil embargo on the United States and some other Western nations. The embargo, a protest against the Western nations' support of Israel in ongoing Arab-Israeli hostilities, lasted through March 1974 and caused a massive increase in America's domestic oil prices. At the height of the crisis, the retail price of a gallon of gasoline rose from 30 cents a gallon to about $1.20. Usually, people didn't spend too much time thinking about the price of gas. However, when prices increased suddenly, as they did in 1973, Americans began to debate what drives gas prices and how to reduce them. As the 1973 experience illustrates, the nation's vulnerability to OPEC policies is often the center of this debate.

OPEC, formed in 1960, is a group of oil producing nations located mainly in the Middle East. The organization produces 40 percent of the world's oil supply. According to the U.S. Energy Information Administration, in 2004 OPEC oil accounted for 44 percent of U.S. oil imports. The OPEC cartel was formed in order to give its members greater leverage in setting the price of oil worldwide. Twice every year, the cartel holds meetings to assign oil output quotas for its members. By restricting output in this way, OPEC ensures that the market does not become flooded with oil, thus keeping oil prices at a competitive level.

Whether or not the United States can do anything about OPEC's price fixing is the subject of heated debate. Some experts argue that the United States should put more pressure on OPEC to increase its output so that oil prices will be lowered for consumers. For example, Oregon senator Ron Wyden argues that the United States should "aggressively pressure OPEC" to increase its oil output. Wyden maintains, "Every president should be willing to stand up to OPEC and the Saudis to protect American consumers from higher gas prices." However, other analysts maintain that confronting OPEC is futile because in the past the organization has simply ignored U.S. demands. According to Adam Sieminski, global oil strategist for Deutsche Bank in London, "Jawboning OPEC doesn't really do a lot of good. The last few times U.S. administration officials have complained about OPEC's behavior, I don't think it's been particularly helpful."

The 1973 increase in gas prices was an anomaly, but since then there have been numerous smaller oil price spikes in the United States, each one prompting concern and public debate over how to reduce prices. While the influence of OPEC is definitely an important contributor, there are many other factors influencing the price of oil in the United States. In the following chapter the authors offer various opinions on what drives oil prices and the best way to reduce them.

> "As a consequence of inadequate domestic refining capacity, approximately 10 percent of America's finished gasoline . . . is shipped in."

America Needs More Oil Refineries

Ben Lieberman

In the following viewpoint Ben Lieberman argues that strict environmental regulations have made building new oil refineries in the United States too costly. As a result, he maintains, existing refineries are operating at capacity and cannot increase production. While the United States is currently forced to import some of its gasoline, federal gasoline regulations are also making this recourse increasingly difficult, says Lieberman. He believes that these factors are likely to cause higher gas prices in the future. Lieberman is a senior policy analyst at the Roe Institute for Economic Policy Studies at the Heritage Foundation. He specializes in the Clean Air Act, climate change, and the impact of environmental policy on energy prices.

As you read, consider the following questions:

1. According to Lieberman, when was the last domestic refinery built?

2. In the author's opinion, what shows that refinery expansions have barely kept up with rising demand?

Asay. © 2005 by Creators Syndicate, Inc. Reproduced by permission.

3. Which region of the country is most dependent on foreign gasoline supplies, according to Lieberman?

Everyone knows that America imports more than half of the oil it uses, but few are aware that the nation also imports some of its gasoline. As a consequence of inadequate domestic refining capacity, approximately 10 percent of America's finished gasoline (and refined gasoline components) is shipped in from Canada, Venezuela, the Caribbean, and Europe. While the need for "energy independence" is often overblown, in this case the growing reliance on foreign refineries does not bode well for the future price of gasoline.

No New Refineries

Despite steadily increasing demand for gasoline and diesel fuel in the US, the last domestic refinery was built in 1976. One reason is the substantial regulatory barriers and costs involved in constructing a new plant and operating it in compliance with the applicable Clean Air Act (CAA) regulations. With regard to the latter, the CAA places a double burden on refiners—strict motor fuel requirements that make gasoline more difficult to produce, and a slew of tough restrictions on refinery emissions. Even with today's high gas prices and strong industry margins, no serious proposal for a new refinery is on the drawing board, and few expect one any time soon.

Until recently, most of the slack has been taken up by capacity expansions at existing refineries. But this has not been easy either, and in fact was made more difficult since 1999 as a result of a Clinton administration crackdown on numerous refiners, claiming violations of the CAA.

Refinery utilization rates hover around 95 percent, very high for any industry. This is a sign that expansions have barely kept up with rising demand. And even that may no longer be true. "Refinery capacity has not expanded significantly since last summer [2003]," according to a recent report by the Department of Energy's Energy Information Administration (EIA).

The Role of Foreign Refineries

Enter foreign refiners, who have been serving American markets for years but who now play a vital and growing role providing Americans with the additional gasoline that domestic refineries cannot. These refiners have the advantage of operating free of the CAA's requirements, though their products must meet all US specifications. As much as 25 percent of the Northeast's gasoline comes from abroad, making it the region most dependent on foreign supplies.

But, just as America is placing increased reliance on non-US refiners, some of those refiners are no longer up to the task. The reason is that federal gasoline requirements continue to get more complicated. In addition to the regulations already in place, the EPA [Environmental Protection Agency] is almost constantly phasing in new ones, such as the low sulfur requirements for motor fuels that took effect at the beginning of [2004]. As the US goes further and further down the path of complex, mandate-laden gasoline recipes, fewer offshore refiners are willing to make the investments necessary to produce these specialized blends. By one estimate reported in *The Houston Chronicle*, the new sulfur standards have taken as much as 150,000 barrels a day off the market, a small fraction of the 9 million barrels America uses each day but enough to make a difference when the market is already tight.

Higher Prices in the Future

Looking ahead to summer [2004], EIA forecasts a slight increase in imports that will only partially satisfy sharply higher demand, as compared to last summer. EIA concludes that "incremental foreign supplies may be hard to come by and are expected to be costly." This could contribute to higher summertime prices, particularly in the Northeast.

Looking even further out, EIA forecasts that demand for petroleum products will increase by 1.6 percent annually for the next 25 years. This fuel will have to be refined somewhere, but where and how is hard to fathom given the current trends.

> *"Domestic gasoline production has actually increased by 20 percent since the last oil refinery was built in 1976."*

America Does Not Need More Oil Refineries

Jerry Taylor and Peter Van Doren

The cause of high gas prices is not the result of a lack of domestic refining capacity, argue Jerry Taylor and Peter Van Doren in the following viewpoint. According to the authors, production at existing refineries has become more efficient, and gasoline imports have become cheaper. In consequence, the United States does not need new oil refineries, they maintain. The price of gasoline is set by the global marketplace, they believe, which the U.S. government can do little about. Taylor is director of natural resource studies at the Cato Institute, a nonprofit, public policy research foundation in Washington, D.C. Van Doren is editor of Cato's Regulation *magazine.*

As you read, consider the following questions:

1. In the authors' opinion, why were there numerous small refineries back in 1981?
2. Why does the United States import gasoline from European refineries, according to Taylor and Van Doren?
3. According to the authors, of the $4 billion to $6 billion

cost of a new oil refinery, how much pays for complying with environmental regulations?

So what's driving these high gasoline prices, which now [in June 2005] average $2.22 across the country? Conservatives think it's largely a function of the chickens coming home to roost. In short, bureaucratic red tape, anti-growth environmental extremists, and "not-in-my-back-yard" community activists have long prevented new oil refineries from coming online. This in turn has starved the market of the gasoline and—*voila!*—record prices are the logical result.

It's a convenient story line for the Right. Unfortunately, the narrative is wrong.

Closing Inefficient Refineries

How can that be, you might ask, when we're constantly beaten around the head with the fact that no new oil-refining plants have been built in the U.S. since 1976? The reason that no new facilities have been built is partly because it costs far less to expand production capacity at existing plants than it does to expand capacity by building new plants. And because existing refineries are ideally situated near oil terminals and pipelines, it's more convenient to increase capacity in those locations than to do so elsewhere.

But if that's so, how do we explain the facility shutdowns that have characterized the industry? After all, there were 325 oil refineries in the U.S. in 1981, but only 149 remain today. The explanation resides in the fact that we had a lot of refineries back in 1981 not because of market forces or the lack of environmental regulations, but because the government subsidized the existence of small, inefficient refineries.

Here's how it worked. Under the Mandatory Oil Import Quota Program (which was in effect from 1959 to 1973), low-cost crude oil imports were restricted to support the domestic crude price. Refineries got disproportionately more rights to

---

Expanding Refining Capacity

While some refineries have closed, and no new refineries have been built in nearly 30 years, many existing refineries have expanded their capacities. As a result of capacity creep, whereby existing refineries create additional refining capacity from the same physical structure, capacity per operating refinery increased by 28% over the 1990 to 1998 period, for example. Overall, since the mid-1990s, U.S. refinery capacity has increased from 15.0 million bbl/d [billion barrels per day] in 1994 to 16.9 million bbl/d in September 2004. Also in September 2004, utilization of operating capacity at U.S. refineries was averaging around 90%, down from 97% in July and August.

U.S. Energy Information Administration, January 2005.
www.eia.doe.gov.

---

import if they were small. The subsidies to small refineries continued under the price-control programs in place from 1973 through 1980. When the subsidies ended, a large number of inefficient small refineries bit the dust.

More Efficient Production

That helps explain why domestic refining capacity dropped from 18.6 million barrels of oil a day in 1976 to 16.8 million barrels of oil today. Dramatic improvements in the operational efficiency of oil refineries also contributed to that decline. Refineries now operate much closer to their capacity than 20 years ago. Accordingly, less "nameplate capacity" is necessary to meet demand.

The upshot is that even though domestic refineries have been shutting down and total refining capacity has been declining, domestic gasoline production has actually *increased* by 20 percent since the last oil refinery was built in 1976.

Cheaper Gasoline Imports

But even that figure only tells part of the story. Gasoline markets today are increasingly global rather than regional in nature. For example, European governments tax diesel fuels less than gasoline and European motorists have responded by using diesel. Accordingly, European refineries make more gasoline than they can use and it's cheaper for us to import that gasoline than to produce it here at home.

The increase in gasoline imports since 1976 (from 2 percent of the market then, to 5.8 percent now) is often cited as evidence that "we have a problem." Nonsense. International trade is a good thing. The more globalized the market, the more diversified our supply and the less vulnerable the U.S. market is to disruption. Morcover, the more global the market, the greater the competition. How much *domestic* refining capability we have is increasingly less important than the amount of international refining capacity we can access.

Government Is Not to Blame

It is true that there is a little slack in production capacity at the moment. Why don't we have more production capacity? Because profit margins in the refining business have traditionally been rather meager. The gasoline refining market is about as close to the model of "perfect competition" as you're going to find outside of an economics textbook. Rents are competed away and little profit is left for producers, especially when compared to the profits available from investment in oil production.

Conservatives believe that environmental regulations have a lot to do with those low profits. They're wrong. A large oil refinery costs $4 billion to $6 billion to build. The installation of "best available control technology" is a very small part of that figure.

Accordingly, President [George W.] Bush's proposals to provide low-cost real estate in the boonies and to somewhat reduce plant costs through regulatory improvements simply won't result in any new refining capacity. We'd love to blame big government and enviro-whackos for today's high gasoline prices (we do, after all, work for the Cato Institute). But telling fairy tales about the market does no one any favors. Prices are high because of global supply-and-demand factors, and Congress can do little about it.

> *"If . . . predictions of 10.3 billion barrels of oil are correct, . . . the American people will have the benefit of that increased domestic oil supply for at least another 30 years."*

Oil Drilling Should Be Allowed in the Arctic National Wildlife Refuge

Walter J. Hickel

Alaska's Arctic National Wildlife Refuge (ANWR) includes areas believed to contain large oil reserves. However, its status as a federal wildlife refuge has made it illegal to explore or drill for oil there, and efforts by Congress to open parts of ANWR for drilling have failed to pass as of the beginning of 2006. In the following viewpoint Walter J. Hickel maintains the United States should open ANWR for drilling in order to reduce America's dependency on foreign sources of petroleum. He argues that oil exploration will not cause great harm to the natural environment. Hickel, a former two-time governor of Alaska, served as U.S. secretary of the interior from 1969 to 1974.

As you read, consider the following questions:

1. What lesson should Americans learn from Hurricane Katrina, according to Hickel?

2. How big an area is under consideration for oil drilling and exploration, according to the author?

3. According to Hickel, which groups of people support ANWR oil exploration?

On September 13 [2005], Jimmy Carter wrote an article for the *Washington Post* on the Arctic National Wildlife Refuge titled "Arctic Folly." While I respect the former President, I strongly disagree with his position on ANWR.

Hurricane Katrina[1] has already taught America much about our nation, including our energy vulnerability. That one storm removed 1 million barrels of oil a day from America's lifelines, contributing to the previously unimaginable price of $65 per barrel of oil, the skyrocketing price of gasoline at the pump, and two airlines declaring bankruptcy. That terrible act of God took us by surprise, and we need to learn from it.

One lesson is to use the natural resources God gave America to meet our own needs and to stop relying on the fuel shipped from abroad, especially from developing nations where it is being ripped from lands and seas with little heed for the environment.

The first, and most obvious step, is to encourage Congress to open the most environmentally protected and promising oil province in North America: the coastal plain of ANWR. This issue is reaching the boiling point, heated by the hurricane, the high price of oil and environmental fears fed mostly by misinformation. . . .

Past Oil Exploration

For the past 60 years, I have watched or participated in the decisions regarding Alaska's sweeping coastal plain. In 1967, as governor of Alaska, I insisted that Atlantic Richfield continue drilling at the North Slope when it announced plans to pull

1. The August 2005 storm destroyed much of America's oil drilling and refining capacity on the Gulf Coast.

out. "You drill, or I will," was my threat. They heard me, drilled at Prudhoe Bay, and discovered the largest oil field in U.S. history, just 55 miles to the west of ANWR.

In 1970, as U.S. secretary of the Interior, I launched the environmental studies that led to the authorization of the trans-Alaska pipeline. Those fields and that remarkable pipeline allow millions of Americans today to fill their gas tanks and heat their homes with energy produced in the U.S. Without Alaska oil, dependency on foreign imports would rise well above today's 60% of U.S. daily consumption.

At issue is oil exploration in the so-called "1002 area," one-eighth of the 19-million-acre Arctic Refuge, most of which is set aside permanently from resource development. This small segment of the coastal plain, however, has long been recognized as the most promising untapped oil province in North America. In 1980, Congress mandated it be studied in depth. The intent was to open the coastal plain carefully and responsibly, not to lock it up. Unfortunately, since then, Congress has been intimidated by political pressure from the domestic environmental movement and its political spokesmen.

The studies of ANWR have long been complete, and Congress is ready to move forward to allow exploration to begin, but it needs public support. From an Alaskan point of view, we find it difficult to understand the opposition, especially from those otherwise credible national figures who are willing to stretch the truth. Scarcer than domestic energy, it appears, is domestic integrity.

Meanwhile, the public is victim to a bumper sticker debate. Who then should you believe? The most credible views are those of the Inupiat Eskimo who have lived on the coastal plain for thousands of years and have co-existed with and benefited from oil development; the biologists who have studied our Arctic wildlife for two generations; and the engineers who have designed the least disruptive oil development procedures in the world. The vast majority of these people believe

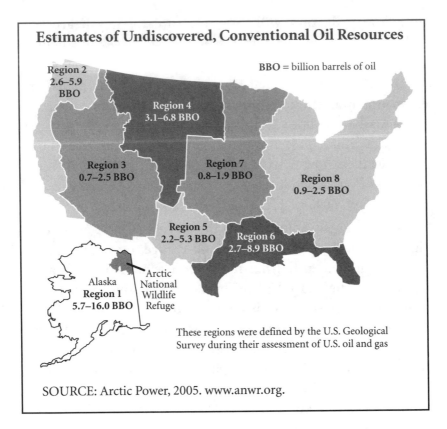

Estimates of Undiscovered, Conventional Oil Resources

BBO = billion barrels of oil

Region 2
2.6–5.9
BBO

Region 4
3.1–6.8 BBO

Region 3
0.7–2.5 BBO

Region 7
0.8–1.9 BBO

Region 8
0.9–2.5 BBO

Region 5
2.2–5.3 BBO

Region 6
2.7–8.9 BBO

Alaska
Region 1
5.7–16.0 BBO

Arctic
National
Wildlife
Refuge

These regions were defined by the U.S. Geological
Survey during their assessment of U.S. oil and gas

SOURCE: Arctic Power, 2005. www.anwr.org.

that oil can be developed on the coastal plain without seriously disturbing the wildlife, and they know what ANWR oil can do for America.

Key Facts About Drilling

Here are key facts about North Slope drilling:

- Did you know most wildlife in the 1002 area are present for only six weeks each year? If you were to fly over the area today, you would find it difficult to spot any animals at all in what the environmental community claims is "America's Serengeti—our pre-eminent wildlife sanctuary." And if you were to fly over it during the eight months of winter when temperatures drop to −70 degrees, you would see even less.

- Did you know North Slope drilling is conducted only in winter to avoid disturbing the summer wildlife populations and will be strictly prohibited in ANWR during the caribou calving season from mid-May to mid-June?

- Did you know Prudhoe Bay is the most environmentally responsible oil field in the world? It is certainly the best I have seen, and I have toured the oil patches in all continents but South America.

- Did you know Prudhoe Bay oil production has operated for 28 years with minimal impact on the wildlife, including the resident Central caribou herd that has grown from 6,000 to 32,000 animals?

- Did you know not a single wildlife species has decreased in population at Prudhoe over this period? Not one caribou has even been killed or harmed by any oil field activity in more than 30 years of human activity at the Prudhoe Bay oil field.

- Did you know the Environmental Protection Agency, the U.S. Fish and Wildlife Service and state agencies such as Environmental Protection and Fish and Game are required by law to monitor industrial activity in Alaska, and they do an outstanding job insuring that wildlife and habitat are protected?

If oil is discovered in the 1002 area and the predictions of 10.3 billion barrels of oil are correct, the trans-Alaska pipeline can return to full capacity, doubling its current production to 2 million barrels a day, and the American people will have the benefit of that increased domestic oil supply for at least another 30 years.

Benefits for America

This will help the U.S. energy-wise and security-wise. As the largest oil-consuming nation, it will make us more credible in terms of the global environment. And it will give us some breathing room as we dedicate our creativity and resources to develop alternative energy sources—an absolute must for the next generation.

> "[In a decade] demand in the United States will be so high that the country will ... have to import ... only four per cent less than if the refuge were left untouched."

Oil Drilling Should Not Be Allowed in the Arctic National Wildlife Refuge

Elizabeth Kolbert

The Arctic National Wildlife Refuge (ANWR), located in north-eastern Alaska, is home to a great variety of wildlife. The area is also believed to contain large oil reserves, and there have been numerous unsuccessful attempts to get Congress to approve drilling for oil there. In the following viewpoint Elizabeth Kolbert argues that drilling in ANWR is not the solution to fulfilling America's energy needs. Oil from ANWR would not contribute significantly to satisfying U.S. demand, she says. Instead, maintains Kolbert, the United States needs to begin reducing its oil consumption. Kolbert is a political correspondent for the weekly New Yorker *magazine.*

As you read, consider the following questions:

1. Why does ANWR land along the Beaufort Sea need protecting, according to Kolbert?

2. According to Kolbert, how will drilling in ANWR impact America's need to import oil?

3. As argued by the author, what would be the result of raising fuel-efficiency standards to forty miles per gallon?

The act that designated the Arctic National Wildlife Refuge was signed into law on December 2, 1980, by President Jimmy Carter, just a few weeks before he left office. It already had a long and troubled history. The act had taken nearly a decade to negotiate, and during this period Carter had been vilified in Anchorage and burned in effigy in Fairbanks. Meanwhile, even though the overarching purpose of the act was supposed to be conservation—the Arctic Refuge is only a small part of the more than a hundred million acres it set aside—by the time it worked its way through Congress it was riddled with parochial and environmentally dubious provisions such as subsidies for logging in national forests. The act's treatment of the refuge itself was particularly equivocal. Some eighteen million acres of mountainous and inaccessible terrain were declared off limits to development. But the land that actually needed protection—one and a half million acres of caribou calving grounds along the Beaufort Sea—was left in legislative limbo. A future Congress could study that area's oil and gas potential and then, if it wished, authorize drilling.

The result of this arrangement has been a battle as long and, up until now, at least, as ineffectual as any on Capitol Hill. The acres left up for grabs in 1980 are often referred to as the "1002 area," after the section of the bill that dealt—or, rather, failed to deal—with their fate. In 1987, President Reagan recommended drilling in the 1002, but Congress rejected the idea. In 1995, Congress authorized opening the area, only to be thwarted by President Clinton. Picking up where Reagan had left off, President George W. Bush, in 2001, included a drilling provision in his ill-fated energy bill; after that bill died, Senate Republicans tried, unsuccessfully, to insert a simi-

The High Risk of Oil Spills

Thousands of caribou and other types of wildlife will be displaced if DC lawmakers pass a measure to allow drilling in the Arctic National Wildlife Refuge (ANWR).

But there's an even bigger issue: the very real possibility of an environmental tragedy as catastrophic as the 1989 oil spill caused by the *Exxon Valdez* oil tanker. Swift measures are needed to address the severe safety and maintenance issues plaguing drilling operations in nearby Prudhoe Bay—North America's biggest oil field, 60 miles west of ANWR—and other areas on Alaska's North Slope....

Chuck Hamel, an Alexandria, Virginia oil industry watchdog, has been leading the fight for the past 15 years against shoddy crude oil operations in Alaska by BP [British Petroleum], ConocoPhillips, and ExxonMobil....

Hamel, who is protecting the identities of the current whistleblowers, says not only do oil spills continue on the North Slope, but the oil behemoth's executives routinely lie to Alaskan state representatives and members of Congress about the steps they're taking to correct problems.

Jason Leopold, Earth Island Journal, *Autumn 2005.*

lar provision into the 2004 budget resolution. Last month, this tactic finally worked, and the Senate approved a budget that would open up the 1002 area. The House of Representatives, however, has not passed the same budget, so the fate of the refuge is now tangled up with a great number of other issues, including Medicaid funding, which have nothing to do with it but which will determine whether or not the two houses can agree on a spending plan. Perversely, one of the key votes in favor of drilling for oil in Alaska came from Senator Mel Martinez, Republican of Florida, who backed it in return for a promise from the Bush Administration to extend a moratorium on drilling for oil in the eastern Gulf of Mexico. ("I would understand how some might view it as a problem," Martinez said of this deal.)

Over the past few weeks, Administration officials have been lobbying hard in favor of opening the refuge. In a speech in Columbus, Ohio, President Bush claimed that drilling operations would be limited to an area the size of that city's airport, and would eventually produce enough crude to "reduce our dependence on foreign oil by up to a million barrels of oil a day." In TV appearances and op-ed pieces, Interior Secretary Gale Norton has sounded similar themes, arguing, on the one hand, that drilling will have almost no impact on wildlife— "The overall 'footprint' of the equipment and facilities needed to develop the 1002 area would be restricted to two thousand acres," she wrote last month in the *Times*—and, on the other, that it is an essential part of "a comprehensive energy strategy." At this point, it would be hard to say which part of the Administration's argument—attempting to minimize drilling's environmental impact or to maximize its strategic significance—is more misleading. (To get to the two-thousand-acre figure, you have to be willing to consider the "footprint" of, say, thirty miles' worth of pipeline as just the area where the pipeline's supports touch the ground.)

No one really knows how much oil lies under the 1002 area; a standard estimate is that seven and a half billion barrels are "technically recoverable." (Some of the oil may be so expensive to extract that recovery isn't economically feasible.) For most countries, a reserve of this size would represent a significant supply. Such is the United States' thirst for petroleum, however, that seven and a half billion barrels is but a tastevin to a wino. The federal Energy Information Administration [E.I.A.] recently predicted that, if drilling is approved this year crude could begin to flow from the Arctic Refuge in a decade, and production would peak, at around eight hundred and seventy-five thousand barrels a day, a dozen years later. The E.I.A. also anticipates that by then demand in the United States will be so high that the country will still have to import sixty-six per cent of its oil, only four per cent less than if the refuge were left untouched.

With or without drilling in the Arctic Refuge, global oil production is expected to start dropping sometime in the next several years, owing to dwindling reserves. A forward-looking energy plan would address this eventuality. Oil consumption in the United States has been steadily rising since Jimmy Carter left office, in 1981. If during that time fuel-efficiency standards for cars and light trucks had been raised by just five miles per gallon, we would now be using one and a half million barrels of oil less each day, and if they had been raised by ten miles per gallon we would be using two and a half million barrels of oil less each day. If fuel-efficiency standards were raised to forty miles per gallon—a level that is eminently achievable with current technology—the United States would save sixty billion barrels of oil over the next fifty years. Simply upgrading the standards for replacement tires so that they match those for tires on new cars would avert the need for seven billion barrels, which is roughly the same amount we could hope to get out of the Arctic Refuge.

So clear are the numbers that just about everyone—outside the White House and Capitol Hill—recognizes what's needed. Recently, a group of military experts sent the President a letter urging him, as a matter of national security, to launch "a major new initiative to curtail U.S. consumption." One signatory, Frank Gaffney, the head of the Center for Security Policy, told the *Wall Street Journal* that reducing oil demand is "no longer a nice thing to do—it's imperative." Preserving the Arctic National Wildlife Refuge won't, of course, do anything to change energy use. But energy policy is no excuse for destroying it.

"The main culprits in the rising gas prices ... [are] the American people who support policies that block new drilling."

America's Domestic Policies Cause High Oil Prices

Tom DeWeese

In the following viewpoint Tom DeWeese blames overly strict domestic policies for America's high gas prices. As a result of environmental campaigns, Americans refuse to support policies allowing increased domestic drilling or the construction of new oil refineries, says DeWeese. This stance is unrealistic, he maintains, considering that at the same time, the population continues to use increasing amounts of oil. He argues that new policies must be implemented to allow America to meet its increasing demand for oil. DeWeese is the publisher and editor of the DeWeese Report *and president of the American Policy Center.*

As you read, consider the following questions:

1. In DeWeese's opinion, why will America's national bird soon be the ostrich instead of the noble eagle?

2. According to the author, what percentage of oil reserves is locked away on federal lands?

3. Why is investment in alternative energy sources "a coward's game," as argued by DeWeese?

Prices at gas pumps are at some of the highest levels ever this summer [2004] and Americans want answers. In particular they want the names and numbers of those to blame. To answer that question perhaps they should simply consult the phone book or look in the mirror. Because the main culprits in the rising gas prices aren't necessarily members of OPEC [Organization of the Petroleum Exporting Countries], but the American people who support policies that block new drilling and the building of new refineries. It's that simple.

The real political parties in America are the NIMBYs (Not In My Back Yard) and the BANANAs (Build Absolutely Nothing Anywhere Near Anything). These two political forces are driving the future of the nation by dictating the policy agendas of the Republicans and Democrats. Soon, the national bird will no longer be the noble eagle, but the ostrich.

"Silly Children"

Americans are becoming adolescent children who want towns to remain small as they themselves have children who must have schools, jobs and homes of their own. They want to build their homes in rural areas with beautiful vistas and complain when someone else wants to do the same thing.

They argue that a neighbor's new home has blocked their "view shed," never considering that their home used to be someone else's view shed or open space. Americans support programs to lock away land to keep wilderness pristine, free of human development, power lines and cell towers. Yet they want to use their cell phones and computers wherever they go. They want three-car garages to house the family van, the daughter's little bug and the husband's sports car; but don't blight the landscape with filling stations, refineries or power plants.

There's no place in our pretty, clean, politically correct, well-ordered world for industry to make the things we need yet, when all of our toys don't work, Americans are outraged and they want heads to roll. Fix it!

Yes, what silly children Americans have become. Yet one can hardly blame the results of two decades of implementing the radical agendas of special interests like the Sierra Club and The Nature Conservancy. These rich and powerful groups have spent billions of dollars to push their agenda of no growth (called Sustainable Development) through Congress and to indoctrinate the rest of us to feel guilty about our very existence. We're sorry we need to use energy. We're sorry that we have to grow food to eat. We're sorry that we keep inventing creature comforts for ourselves.

The answer from a sorry society, while not giving up our toys, is to just ban the building of the things that make them work. It all sounds so noble. We pack public meetings to express our outrage over the idea of building a power plant in the community. We certainly don't want that smelly thing around here! Did you know that new cell tower would interfere with the view of the historic battlefield? General Robert E. Lee didn't see that tower during the battle, so it must be banned. Just get on your cell phone and call everyone you know to come to the meeting and oppose it. And also, make sure you let them know that we are all properly indignant about those evil developers trying to build more houses. Tell everyone in your new neighborhood to join our protest.

Such is today's modern American society. We are indeed properly indignant with no responsibility for the consequences. Now the chickens are indeed coming home to roost. Energy we so desperately need to run our homes, cars, airplanes, and industry can't be produced fast enough. As a result, the cost of heating and cooling our homes, driving our cars, and flying our planes is spinning out of control.

Overzealous Environmental Regulation

88% of the energy for America's transportation, industry, government, and residential needs comes from oil, gas, and coal.

Without them the nation shuts down. Yet there is no drive in Congress to ease regulations to allow for domestic production.

Through pressure from environmental organizations, Congress and federal agencies have banned oil activity from more than 300 million acres of federal land onshore and more than 460 million acres offshore in the past 20 years. An estimated 67% of oil reserves and 40% of natural gas reserves are locked away on federal lands in America's western states.

Today's domestic oil production comes from a diminishing number of wells scattered throughout the country. The most important discovery of new oil reserves has been in Alaska in the Arctic National Wildlife Reserve (ANWR). Yet, Congress has refused to allow drilling for this urgently needed American resource because of lies told by environmentalists that the drilling will damage the Alaskan ecosystem. Such Green scare-mongering is simply not true.

Instead, Congress plays to the whims of the Greens, NIMBYs and BANANAs by ignoring domestic resources and importing oil from unstable political sources. By doing that, Congress eliminates pressure from highly paid green lobbyists who want the land locked away and sidesteps town meetings with angry citizens who don't want oil wells in their back yards.

No New Refineries

However, the nation's energy problem is much worse than just not being able to drill our American oil. Even if we could drill our own oil or even had a glut of imported oil, the supply crisis couldn't be averted to bring oil prices down. That's because the United States hasn't built a new oil refinery since 1976. All remaining American refineries are running at full capacity. There is barely time for the plants to shut down to perform needed upkeep and repairs because such activity will cause a bump in the system and force prices up. The industry can do nothing to keep up with demand. Rules and regulations, both

A Lopsided Discussion

There will always be environmental activists who fight any new proposed refinery, regardless of where it might be located and how environmentally safe it is. And our environmental rules give them the upper hand. . . .

You wind up with a very lopsided discussion where potential problems are thoroughly and perhaps overly represented, but the only group pointing out the benefits of the refinery is the "evil" oil company asking to build it—even though every automobile driver would benefit.

Adrian Moore, Orange County Register, *September 1, 2005.*

federal and state, are blocking the industry's ability to build new refineries.

Even worse: old, worn out refineries are closing, reducing capacity even more. In California, ten refineries representing 20% of the state's refining capacity were closed between 1985 and 1995. With California energy policy literally dominated by radical environmental groups, it is unlikely that any new refineries will ever be built.

To build a new refinery would take a risk of at least $2 billion in a ten-year undertaking. In the end, even if permits are obtained there is no guarantee that the refinery will ever be built. Nobody wants to invest in new refineries because there is no money to be made. If there were investors willing to take the risk, where would it be built? What town would welcome it? What land would be used? Radical environmentalists are well organized to build pressure on any politician who might support such an endeavor. They know how to energize the NIMBYs and BANANAs. All the greens have to do is voice concerns about air pollution or the dangers of large trucks carrying hazardous materials or the potential for leakage into the environment. Just a hint at these things and poof, the refinery is history. Scientific facts are rarely heard in the din of the argument.

The Department of Energy predicts domestic oil consumption will increase 43 percent by 2025, but production will grow only by 23 percent. So, as our nation's future teeters on the brink, Congress plays a coward's game by producing an energy policy that pours more than $23 billion of taxpayer money into alternative energy sources like windmills, solar panels, and ethanol, all in the name of conservation. The truth is, no combination of conservation, technology or alternative fuels can come close to replacing the fossil fuels system already in place. It will take years for research, testing, permitting, construction and distribution systems for replacement alternatives to be realized. Meanwhile, we need oil and gas now! . . .

Bold Policies Are Needed

Now is the time (in fact we are way past time) to put a long-term plan in place with bold policies to keep the nation's lights on and transportation and industry moving. It must include opening access to energy-rich areas currently off limits for exploration. Such areas include offshore sites and the Outer Continental Shelf, and the mere 2,000 acres in ANWR.

Typically, as the nation's urgently needed resources are locked away and the existing oil market grows more unstable by the day with prices rising to new heights, our politicians are playing the usual blame game. The Democrats want an investigation of the oil companies to see if they are gouging the consumer, ignoring the fact that the real gougers are federal and state governments which tax every gallon by as much as 50 cents. This is on top of the increased costs of environmental regulations on the oil industry.

Predictably, the environmentalists are revving up their campaigns against SUV's [sport utility vehicles] as they propose more and more draconian conservation programs that are designed to get Americans out of their cars. Meanwhile, the Bush Administration is busy applying pressure on OPEC to produce more oil that we have no capacity to refine. No one is talking about real solutions.

The United States plays dumb as the Middle East grows ever more dangerous and unstable. We have allowed ourselves no running room, no bargaining chip, and no alternative should the region completely implode into terrorist anarchy. Our economy would quickly resemble the World Trade Center [after the September 11, 2001, terrorist attacks] and our national security would face severe threat. Energy has become the molten lava of an inferno burning just under the surface of the U.S. economy, which is primed for meltdown.

So oil prices continue to rise as demand increases and supply gets locked away in a national park, or bottlenecked in an ever-shrinking number of American refineries. Our elected representatives play silly games. Environmentalists relentlessly push their anti-civilization agenda. And the indignant NIMBYs and BANANAs continue to sleep, satisfied that their world is well controlled.

> "We remain dependent on oil from the Mideast . . . because extracting oil from the deserts of the Persian Gulf is so easy and cheap."

Reliance on Middle East Oil Keeps Oil Prices High

Peter Huber and Mark Mills

High oil prices are not the result of worldwide oil depletion, maintain Peter Huber and Mark Mills in the following viewpoint. Instead, the authors argue, oil prices are high because Saudi Arabia controls so much of the market that it can charge whatever it wants for oil. The authors contend that Saudi Arabia charges wildly fluctuating oil prices, corresponding to the tumultuous political events that constantly plague the nation. Despite this, Huber and Mills point out, oil is still cheaper to extract in Saudi Arabia, so other nations have not invested in domestic drilling operations and remain vulnerable to Saudi Arabian price-gouging. Huber and Mills are coauthors of The Bottomless Well: The Twilight of Fuel, the Virtue of Waste, and Why We Will Never Run Out of Energy.

As you read, consider the following questions:

1. According to Huber and Mills, what is the current cost of extracting oil in Saudi Arabia?

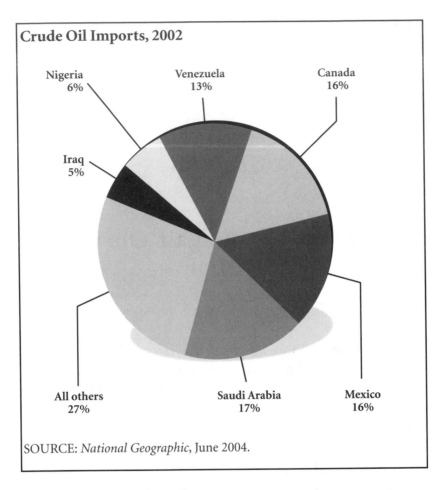

Crude Oil Imports, 2002

Nigeria 6%
Venezuela 13%
Canada 16%
Iraq 5%
All others 27%
Saudi Arabia 17%
Mexico 16%

SOURCE: *National Geographic*, June 2004.

2. How much oil is there in Venezuela's Orinoco Basin, and Alberta's Athabasca sands, in the authors' opinion?

3. How could Saudi Arabia force a complete write-off of investment in Venezuelan and Canadian oil, as explained by Huber and Mills?

The price of oil remains high only because the cost of oil remains so low. We remain dependent on oil from the Mideast not because the planet is running out of buried hydrocarbons, but because extracting oil from the deserts of the Persian Gulf is so easy and cheap that it's risky to invest capital to extract somewhat more stubborn oil from far larger deposits in Alberta.

The market price of oil is indeed hovering up around $50-a-barrel on the spot market. But getting oil to the surface currently costs under $5 a barrel in Saudi Arabia, with the global average cost certainly under $15. And with technology already well in hand, the cost of sucking oil out of the planet we occupy simply will not rise above roughly $30 per barrel for the next 100 years at least.

Finding and Extracting

The cost of oil comes down to the cost of finding, and then lifting or extracting. First, you have to decide where to dig. Exploration costs currently run under $3 per barrel in much of the Mideast, and below $7 for oil hidden deep under the ocean. But these costs have been falling, not rising, because imaging technology that lets geologists peer through miles of water and rock improves faster than supplies recede. Many lower-grade deposits require no new looking at all.

To pick just one example among many, finding costs are essentially zero for the 3.5 trillion barrels of oil that soak the clay in the Orinoco basin in Venezuela, and the Athabasca tar sands in Alberta, Canada. Yes, that's [3.5] trillion—over a century's worth of global supply, at the current 30-billion-barrel-a-year rate of consumption.

Then you have to get the oil out of the sand—or the sand out of the oil. In the Mideast, current lifting costs run $1 to $2.50 per barrel at the very most; lifting costs in Iraq probably run closer to 50 cents, though OPEC [Organization of the Petroleum Exporting Countries] strains not to publicize any such embarrassingly low numbers. For the most expensive offshore platforms in the North Sea, lifting costs (capital investment plus operating costs) currently run comfortably south of $15 per barrel. Tar sands, by contrast, are simply strip mined, like western coal, and that's very cheap—but then you spend another $10, or maybe $15, separating the oil from the dirt. To do that, oil or gas extracted from the site itself is burned to heat water, which is then used to "crack" the bitumen from the clay; the bitumen is then chemically split to produce lighter petroleum.

In sum, it costs under $5 per barrel to pump oil out from under the sand in Iraq, and about $15 to melt it out of the sand in Alberta. So why don't we just learn to love hockey and shop Canadian? Conventional Canadian wells already supply us with more oil than Saudi Arabia, and the Canadian tar is now delivering, too. The $5 billion (U.S.) Athabasca Oil Sands Project that Shell and ChevronTexaco opened in Alberta [in 2004] is now pumping 155,000 barrels per day. And to our south, Venezuela's Orinoco Belt yields 500,000 barrels daily.

Saudi Arabia's Abundance

But here's the catch: By simply opening up its spigots for a few years, Saudi Arabia could, in short order, force a complete write-off of the huge capital investments in Athabasca and Orinoco. Investing billions in tar-sand refineries is risky not because getting oil out of Alberta is especially difficult or expensive, but because getting oil out of Arabia is so easy and cheap. Oil prices gyrate and occasionally spike—both up and down—not because oil is scarce, but because it's so abundant in places where good government is scarce. Investing $5 billion dollars over five years to build a new tar-sand refinery in Alberta is indeed risky when a second cousin of [terrorist] Osama bin Laden can knock $20 off the price of oil with an idle wave of his hand on any given day in Riyadh [Saudi Arabia].

The one consolation is that Arabia faces a quandary of its own. Once the offshore platform has been deployed in the North Sea, once the humongous crock pot is up and cooking in Alberta, its cost is sunk. The original investors may never recover their capital, but after it has been written off, somebody can go ahead and produce oil very profitably going forward. And capital costs are going to keep falling, because the cost of a tar-sand refinery depends on technology, and technology costs always fall. Bacteria, for example, have already been successfully bioengineered to crack heavy oil molecules to help clean up oil spills, and to mine low-grade copper; bugs could likewise end up trampling out the vintage where the Albertan oil is stored.

No Oil Shortage Ahead

In the short term anything remains possible. Demand for oil grows daily in China and India, where good government is finally taking root, while much of the earth's most accessible oil lies under land controlled by feudal theocracies, kleptocrats, and fanatics. Day by day, just as it should, the market attempts to incorporate these two antithetical realities into the spot price of crude. But to suppose that those prices foreshadow the exhaustion of the planet itself is silly.

The cost of extracting oil from the earth has not gone up over the past century, it has held remarkably steady. Going forward, over the longer term, it may rise very gradually, but certainly not fast. The earth is far bigger than people think, the untapped deposits are huge, and the technologies for separating oil from the planet keep getting better. U.S. oil policy should be to promote new capital investment in the United States, Canada, and other oil-producing countries that are politically stable, and promote stable government in those that aren't.

Periodical Bibliography

The following articles have been selected to supplement the diverse views presented in this chapter.

Donald Coxe — "Why Gas Will Stay Pricey: It's Simple: This time There's No Extra Supply to Sate the Booming Demand," *Maclean's*, July 1, 2004.

Larry E. Craig — "We Must Stabilize Gas Prices with Energy Production," *Human Events*, May 10, 2004.

Cary A. Deck and Bart J. Wilson — "Economics at the Pump: Does 'Anti-Price Gouging' Legislation Really Help Gasoline Consumers?" *Regulation*, Spring 2004.

Lisa W. Drew — "Wilderness Lost: Everyone Knows There's Oil in Alaska's Wildlife Refuge. But That's Only Half the Story," *New Scientist*, April 16, 2005.

Issues and Controversies On File — "Fuel Prices," May 28, 2004.

Jason Leopold — "Alaska's Crude Threat: Oil Spills on the North Slope Are Routine, and So Are Oil Executives' Lies About Them," *Earth Island Journal*, Autumn 2005.

Paul J. Lim, Marianne Lavelle, and Nisha Ramachandran — "Fueling Fears," *U.S. News & World Report*, August 29, 2005.

Mike McNamee and Lorraine Woellert — "You Can't Feed the Oil Monster with a Dixie Cup," *Business Week*, September 12, 2005.

National Review — "Why Are Gasoline Prices on the Rise? Unexpectedly Strong Demand from China and India Is the Main Culprit Driving Higher World Crude Prices," April 19, 2004.

Jeffrey St. Clair — "How the Two Parties Serve Big Oil," *CounterPunch*, September 7–15, 2004.

Mortimer B. Zuckerman — "Getting Real About Gas Prices," *U.S. News & World Report*, April 12, 2004.

OPPOSING
VIEWPOINTS®
SERIES

What Energy Policies Should America Pursue?

Chapter Preface

In 1979 a partial core meltdown occurred at the nuclear power station on Three Mile Island in Pennsylvania. The meltdown occurred over the course of five days, releasing radioactive gas. Although government reports found that no identifiable deaths or injuries occurred as a result, the incident dramatically decreased public support for nuclear power. While other countries such as France and Japan obtain a significant portion of their power from nuclear power stations, since the Three Mile Island accident no nuclear power stations have been constructed in the United States. Recently, however, there is increasing concern that America will not be able to continue relying on oil as its primary source of energy. There are calls to revise the nation's energy policy, decreasing its dependence on oil and pursuing alternative sources of energy. One of these potential sources is nuclear power.

Proponents insist that nuclear power is a safe, reliable, and plentiful energy source. Douglas S. McGregor, director of the Semiconductor Materials and Radiological Technologies Laboratory at the University of Michigan believes that in light of such advantages, nuclear power is a logical choice for America. "The looming specter of a severe energy shortage in this country should spark an increasing demand for nuclear power," he maintains. According to advocates, nuclear power generates far less pollution than other sources of energy. U.S. ambassador John Ritch argues, "The reality is that, of all energy forms capable of meeting the world's expanding energy needs, nuclear power yields the least and most easily managed waste." Advocates like scientist James Lovelock believe that resistance to the use of nuclear power is unfounded. Lovelock insists, "Opposition to nuclear energy is based on irrational fear fed by Hollywood-style fiction, the Green lobbies, and the media.

These fears are unjustified, and nuclear energy from its start in 1952 has proved to be the safest of all energy sources."

However, nuclear power also has many opponents, who contend that this technology is not the answer to America's energy needs. The main fuel used in nuclear reactors is a dense mineral called uranium. According to journalist Michael Parfit, like oil, this mineral will also run out eventually. "The allure is clear: abundant power, no carbon dioxide emissions, no blots on the landscape," he says, "but . . . nuclear power is far from renewable. The readily available uranium fuel won't last much more than 50 years." Many people also believe that nuclear power is not worth the risks it poses to society. Energy expert Cameron M. Burns points out that nuclear power leads to the creation of toxic nuclear waste. "Despite trying for decades and spending billions, the U.S. government has been unable to create safe storage for nuclear plant waste," says Burns, "which stays highly radioactive for thousands of years." Chemist Chris Busby agrees. In his opinion, because of the waste and the potential for accidents, nuclear power poses a high level of risk that outweighs its benefits. He maintains, "The risks to us, to our children and to life on earth the economic, environmental and social costs—are wholly unacceptable."

Nuclear power is not the only energy source that has provoked fierce public debate in the United States. As the debate over energy continues, however, there is increasing agreement on one point: The United States needs to find new ways to meet its increasing energy needs. The following chapter offers various opinions on the question of what energy policies the United States should pursue.

*"Oil dependency threatens our freedom,
safety, and moral values."*

The United States Should Reduce Its Consumption of Foreign Oil

Michael T. Klare

*Michael T. Klare asserts in the following viewpoint that foreign
oil dependency has high financial and environmental costs for
America. He argues that instead of spending money to improve
its highways, which merely encourages more driving, the country
should invest in mass transit and transportation that uses renewable, nonpolluting fuels. Klare is a professor at Hampshire
College in Massachusetts and author of* Blood and Oil: The
Dangers of America's Growing Petroleum Dependency.

As you read, consider the following questions:

1. According to Klare, how much of America's oil consumption is used for transportation?
2. Upon what type of suppliers is the United States increasingly reliant, in the author's opinion?
3. As argued by Klare, how much of America's carbon
   dioxide emissions come from the burning of oil?

Michael T. Klare, "Even Without Accidents, Highways Kill Us: Oil Dependency," www.
minutemanmedia.org, May 18, 2005. Copyright © 2005 by MinutemanMedia.org. Reproduced by permission.

Congress has approved a $284 billion bonanza for highway construction and transportation projects through 2009. This record spending level will no doubt prove immensely popular with America's motorists, mall developers, and construction firms.

But everyone would be better off in the long run if we followed a different path.

Here's a radical yet rational proposal for next year [2006]: spend the $225 billion slated for highways instead on mass transit, high-speed intercity rail, and alternative fuels and energy-efficient vehicles. That revolutionary move would serve the nation's best interests.

Dependence on Foreign Oil

Admittedly, many thoroughfares need work. But the problem here is oil. Every highway improvement boosts motor vehicle use, which increases oil consumption. The more oil we use, the more we depend on foreign suppliers like Saudi Arabia as more dollars spill outside our borders. Meanwhile, our contribution to the buildup of climate-changing gases in the atmosphere spirals out of control.

The U.S. consumes approximately 20 million barrels of oil a day—about 840 million gallons. Most of this, about 70 percent, is used for transportation, primarily by passenger cars, trucks, buses, and other motor vehicles. The nation used to produce most of the oil it consumed. But our domestic output has declined since 1972 and we depend on foreign oil. Today, approximately 55 percent of our oil is imported. That proportion is expected to reach 60 percent in 2010, and to keep rising after that.

If all of our foreign oil came from Britain, Canada, Norway, and other stable, predictably friendly nations, foreign oil dependence wouldn't be a concern—aside from financial implications. But most of the safe foreign suppliers, like those three, are running out of oil. We are becoming increasingly re-

> ## Dangerous Dependence
>
> Almost everyone knows that our dependence on imported oil threatens American security. Ensuring our access to Middle East oil has meant sending troops to unstable countries. Money we spent on oil has ended up funding terrorists. Oil price spikes have preceded every recession in the last 40 years.
>
> *Allan Nogee,* Liberal Opinion Week, *October 11, 2004.*

liant on less stable, often unfriendly suppliers, including Angola, Iraq, Kazakhstan, Nigeria, Russia, Saudi Arabia and Venezuela. These countries alone possess sufficient untapped supplies to satisfy our habit.

Financial Costs of Dependency

Oil dependency threatens our freedom, safety, and moral values. To ensure a steady stream of it, the U.S. has often been compelled to forge questionable alliances with unsavory foreign regimes, such as our shameful commitment to protect the Saudi royal family against all its potential enemies, foreign and domestic. These arrangements force us to grovel before foreign monarchs like the one we rebelled against in 1776, providing them with arms and ammunition.

Our growing foreign energy reliance weakens our currency and economy. Every day, we import approximately 11 million barrels of oil. At the current price of about $50 per barrel, that amounts to a net daily outflow of half a billion dollars—or $200 billion per year. That's one of the largest items in our massive balance-of-payments deficit, and a major factor in the dollar's declining value.

If we keep exporting dollars this way, we will invite a significant economic slowdown, with painful consequences for all Americans.

Environmental Costs of Dependency

Finally, there is the matter of greenhouse-gas emissions. The U.S. is the world's leading emitter of carbon dioxide [CO_2]—the principal source of global climate change. The biggest share of our CO_2 emissions, about 43 percent, comes from the burning of oil. According to the latest Department of Energy projections, our petroleum-related CO_2 emissions will rise by 41 percent between now and 2025, from approximately 2,500 to 3,530 million metric tons.

Let's face it: there's no way that we can reduce our greenhouse-gas emissions and thereby slow the pace of devastating climate change if we continue to burn petroleum at this rate.

Alternatives to Oil

So, instead of spending hundreds of billions of dollars on highways, which encourages increased oil consumption, let's invest in urban mass transit, high-speed intercity rail systems (like those now operating in Europe), and the development of environmentally-friendly energy systems, including those powered by the sun, wind, and waste biomass.

In particular, let's devote a substantial sum—say $50 billion—for accelerating the development of hybrid vehicles, super-fuel-efficient cars, and hydrogen-powered fuel cells. That would reduce our dependence on foreign oil regimes, increase our safety, bolster the economy, slow the pace of climate change, and generate just as many jobs (if not more) than the billions spent on highways.

Despite the inconvenience on the highway, it would be a good deal for America.

> *"Any significant reduction in U.S. demand would hit domestic sources hard but do little to change the amount of foreign oil we buy."*

Reducing Consumption of Foreign Oil Will Harm the United States

Austan Goolsbee

In the following viewpoint Austan Goolsbee maintains that reducing America's dependence on foreign oil would actually cost the nation more money. Since it costs much less to buy oil produced in foreign nations than it does to extract and refine it in America, he notes, the United States saves money by buying foreign oil. Furthermore, Goolsbee maintains, if America reduces its purchasing of foreign oil, global oil prices will fall, making it more difficult for American oil companies to compete. Such an economic hit to one of the nation's major industries would harm the economy, he concludes. Goolsbee is the Robert P. Gwinn Professor of Economics at the University of Chicago and a senior research fellow at the American Bar Foundation.

As you read, consider the following questions:

1. According to the author, how much of its oil does the United States import from OPEC?

2. What are average U.S. oil production costs compared to costs in places like Iran and Saudi Arabia, as explained by Goolsbee?

3. In the author's opinion, why did America's lowest share of foreign oil imports occur in the early 1980s?

Every administration since Richard Nixon's has railed against foreign oil—at least when prices are high. President George W. Bush recently called our dependence on the stuff a "foreign tax on the American dream." Indeed, the promise of energy independence helped the Energy Bill land on President Bush's desk at the end of July [2005].[1] As Senate Majority Leader Bill Frist chimed in, "When we rely on other nations for more than half our oil supply, we simply put our security at risk."

Faulty Reasoning

A basic tenet underlying such comments is that, quite apart from the need to stimulate new domestic energy sources, we must reduce our overall demand for oil if we are to reduce our dependence on foreign sources of the stuff. To that end the bill provides more than $1 billion of subsidies for hybrids and home energy conservation. But there's a problem with this line of thinking. It ignores the way oil pricing really functions, and put simply, it won't work. The costs of pumping oil in the U.S. are among the highest in the world, and the costs in the Middle East are the lowest. So in fact any significant reduction in U.S. demand would hit domestic sources hard but do little to change the amount of foreign oil we buy.

Importance of Extraction Costs

At first glance, weaning the country from foreign oil through conservation seems straightforward. The U.S. imports about 25% of its oil from OPEC [Organization of the Petroleum Ex-

1. This bill, signed by Bush in August 2005, includes incentives for the development of alternative energy technologies.

Myth of Independence

Energy independence for the United States is a myth. . . .

The truth is, the only way America could become energy-independent would be to revert to a 19th-century standard of living.

Charley Reese, Conservative Chronicle, *June 23, 2004.*

porting Countries]. Reduce demand 25%, and we could cut OPEC loose. Though consumer-goods analogies are imperfect, think of the oil market as a bit like going out on a hot day with sodas you bought at the grocery store for 50 cents a can, when they cost $1 a can from a vending machine at the beach. If the grocery store is the domestic supply and the vending machine is the foreign, then reducing demand for soda to the number of cans you brought yourself will end your dependence on foreign soda. But unfortunately, it wouldn't be the OPEC oil we would stop buying if our demand fell. In today's oil market, it's as if the grocery store sodas cost 50 cents but the vending machine sodas cost only 10 cents. In that case, reduce the demand for soda enough, and you will stop buying soda from the grocery store entirely. You would buy cans from the grocery store only if the vending machine couldn't serve all your needs (or if a cartel of vending machines was restricting production, as it were).

In the world of oil, we're the proud sellers of some very high-priced soda. Most oil that was cheap to produce from the U.S. was used up long ago. Today the largest potential sources of oil in North America, be they the shale deposits in Utah and Wyoming, the oil sands of Alberta, or the deep water offshore pools in the Gulf of Mexico, are all much more expensive than the cheap oil coming out of the Middle East. Our average production costs in some places are as high as $15 per barrel. Cost estimates for places like Iran and Saudi Arabia go as low as $1.50 per barrel.

Hurting Domestic Producers

If U.S. demand (which is the largest of any country in the world) falls substantially, it will drive down oil prices. When prices are low, many U.S. oilfields become too expensive to keep open. That is why our lowest share of foreign oil imports in the past three decades came in the early 1980s—when oil shocks drove prices to record highs and encouraged development of the higher-cost U.S. sources.

Without question, driving down oil prices by reducing our demand could reduce the total amount of money going to the Middle East. We should be aware, though, that this reduction will cause far greater damage to the world's high-cost producers of oil, such as those in the U.S. than it does to OPEC, and there is little chance it will reduce the share of our oil that comes from abroad. If we are to seriously contemplate lowering our dependence on foreign oil, we must find a way to reduce the cost of producing alternative energy sources. Hopefully, sources like wind, solar power, or hydrogen fuel cells will eventually get to a point where they become cheaper than fossil fuels. But the sad reality is that while we might be able to cut greenhouse gas emissions by reducing our demand for oil, Bush's "foreign tax on the American dream" is not getting cut anytime soon.

> *"Public opinion strongly supports higher fuel efficiency, and our environment, national, and economic security demand it."*

Fuel Efficiency Standards Should Be Raised

Joan Claybrook

The United States needs to raise its Corporate Average Fuel Economy (CAFE) standards—the laws that regulate fuel economy—argues Joan Claybrook in the following viewpoint. Claybrook believes that the American economy suffers because of its heavy dependence on foreign oil; indeed, after every oil price spike caused by foreign oil producers, the U.S. economy suffers a recession. Claybrook contends that Americans both want and need higher CAFE standards. She maintains that such standards will not cause a decrease in vehicle safety because efficiency can be increased without reducing a vehicle's weight. Claybrook is president of Public Citizen, a national nonprofit public interest organization.

As you read, consider the following questions:

1. According to Claybrook, by how much did CAFE standards raise the fuel economy of the U.S. vehicle fleet between 1978 and 1985?

Joan Claybrook, testimony before the Senate Committee on Commerce, Science, and Transportation, Washington, DC, January 24, 2002.

2. As argued by the author, what percentage of Americans believe that greater conservation of energy supplies is important?

3. According to the DOE, as cited by Claybrook, what type of vehicle improvements caused the majority of fuel economy gains following the 1975 CAFE law?

The Corporate Average Fuel Economy (CAFE) system that was instituted in 1975 is sorely in need of a Congressional upgrade. CAFE, which was crafted in view of the vehicles and technology available at the time, was a smashing success, raising average fuel economy performance for the entire fleet in the U.S. 82 percent between 1978 and 1985. Its primary feature is a 27.5 miles per gallon (mpg) standard for passenger automobiles, set by statute. There is no minimum standard for light trucks, but the National Highway Traffic Safety Administration (NHTSA) is instructed by law to set a standard every year according to what is "maximally feasible."

The Value of CAFE

CAFE currently [in 2002] saves us 118 million gallons of gasoline every day and 913 million barrels of oil each year, or about the total imported annually from the Persian Gulf. It was a major factor in breaking the stranglehold of the Organization of the Petroleum Exporting Countries (OPEC) on oil prices and cutting rampant U.S. inflation in the early 1980s. Since 1985, no major congressional initiative or agency action has been taken to update CAFE standards to reflect current technology, shifting vehicle use, or the need to address global warming and foreign oil dependency. As SUVs [sport utility vehicles] have come to dominate our highways, the American public has recognized that the program is outdated. . . .

Americans do want Congress to require improvements in fuel economy, and consumers are willing to pay for such improvements. . . .

Catrow. © by Copley News Service. Reproduced by permission.

Ninety-three percent of Americans believe the United States should require cars to get better gas mileage to reduce our dependence on foreign oil, and 61 percent believe that greater conservation of energy supplies is an important piece of the solution to our energy problems. In the face of such strong and consistent public opinion over the years favoring significant improvements in fuel economy, it would be irresponsible for Congress not to act [to raise CAFE standards]. . . .

The Myth of the Safety Tradeoff

The auto industry has argued, time and again, that raising fuel economy standards will adversely impact safety by causing the increased production of smaller vehicles or by reducing vehicle weight. In fact, there is no evidence that establishes a clear correlation between vehicle weight and increased fatalities—some heavier cars are far more dangerous to both their occupants and to others on the highway than are lighter ones.

Across many measures of crashworthiness, the newest fuel guzzlers—the SUVs—are the worst performers. What matters most for safety are the crashworthiness protections and the compatibility that is designed and built into vehicles, and these must be enhanced as critical parts of any comprehensive highway safety and fuel economy program.

The use of the time-worn safety canard by industry is a cynical attempt to frighten consumers and Congress in an attempt to deflect new requirements, and appears most appallingly hypocritical when we consider that industry has acted to obstruct safety improvements whenever possible. Industry deploys a misleading safety "red herring" only because it hopes that it will offer a modicum of political cover for its unwillingness to act responsibly. . . .

Fuel Economy and Vehicle Size

Looking at the CAFE-weight relationship . . . as fleet fuel economy increased over time, vehicle weights did not move in any one direction. In 1975, cars weighing less than 2,500 pounds made up 10.8 percent of the new-car fleet, but only 2.6 percent in 2000. By contrast, cars in the over 4,500 pound weight class made up 50 percent of the new-car fleet in 1975 but only 0.9 percent in 2000. These data show that CAFE standards did not cause a uniform reduction in vehicle weight at the light vehicle level (although CAFE may have caused a reduction in average weight, as more cars were built in the 2,500–4,500 pound category). Because automakers could get proportionally more fuel savings from reducing the weight of the heaviest class of cars, those were the first targets for fuel economy improvements, and production numbers for cars in the lightest class actually decreased.

Any improvement in the CAFE standards made today will likely have a similarly small impact on the weight or production levels of the smallest cars. It is not cost-effective to reduce their weights by very much, given the limited fuel economy improvement from doing so and the relatively higher cost of vehicle redesign. . . .

A Department of Energy (DOE) study found that 85 percent of the fuel economy gains made following the 1975 CAFE law were from improvements in vehicle technology rather than weight reduction. The evidence strongly suggests that similar technological leaps are currently available or just around the corner, and that the recent stagnation and even backsliding in overall fuel economy is a trend that must be stopped.

The Union of Concerned Scientists (UCS) pointed out in a report released in 2001 that today's vehicles could become more fuel efficient at a price that would easily be made up in savings on fuel costs, and the necessary changes would have no negative impact on safety. Technologies currently used in portions of today's fleet, if adopted fleetwide, could make vehicles more streamlined, less fuel intensive, and more efficient. . . .

America's Economic Health

Automobile manufacturers have argued that improving fuel economy will cripple their ability to do business by preventing them from giving the customer what she wants. They argue, further, that because the automobile industry is so critical to the health of the American economy it would be destructive to the economy as a whole if Congress were to prescribe new fuel economy standards. Their conclusion shortchanges their own talented engineers and runs contrary to economic history. . . .

Unstable oil and gas prices destabilize the American economy. Each of the three major oil price spikes [during the period of 1972–2002] (1973–74, 1979–80, and 1990–91) was followed by an economic recession in the United States. Because so much of our oil must be imported, we are at the mercy of OPEC and foreign governments should they choose to act to rapidly raise oil prices as they did [in 2000]. Our economy, as it is currently structured, requires the importation of over $100 billion of crude oil and petroleum products each year, which accounts for 29 percent of our trade deficit and totals $378 for every man, woman, and child in the U.S. American spending on gasoline consumption—$186 billion in 2000—renders consumers vulnerable to sudden price spikes over which they have no control.

The economic cost of U.S. oil dependence over the past 30 years has been estimated at $7 trillion dollars of present value—an amount approximately equal to the combined 2000 Gross Domestic Product (GDP) of France, the United Kingdom, Germany and India. If we were to reduce our use of oil substantially, this wealth would remain within the United States and we would have greater control over economic growth. . . .

Public opinion strongly supports higher fuel efficiency, and our environment, national, and economic security demand it. Improvements in fuel economy, vehicle rollover crashworthiness, and reductions in vehicle aggressivity will save both gas and human life.

> "The social costs of raising CAFE standards substantially exceed the social benefits."

Fuel Efficiency Standards Should Not Be Raised

David N. Laband and Christopher Westley

In the following viewpoint David N. Laband and Christopher Westley maintain that raising America's Corporate Average Fuel Economy (CAFE) standards—which regulate vehicle fuel economy—is not the best way to respond to high gas prices. First, they argue, history shows that CAFE standards do not make any difference to gas prices. Second, Laband and Westley assert, raising CAFE standards may actually harm society by leading to higher vehicle costs and the manufacture of lighter, less-safe vehicles. Laband is a professor of economics and policy in the School of Forestry at Auburn University in Alabama. Westley is an assistant professor of economics at Jacksonville State University in Alabama.

As you read, consider the following questions:

1. According to the authors, how do higher gas prices motivate changes in driver behavior?

2. Technologically, in what two ways can car manufactur-

David N. Laband and Christopher Westley, "How *Not* to Respond to Higher Gasoline Prices," *Freeman*, vol. 54, October 2004, pp. 23–24. Copyright 2004 by Foundation for Economic Education, Inc., www.fee.org. All rights reserved. Reproduced by permission.

ers meet higher CAFE standards, according to Laband and Westley?

3. Why are air bags now required in the new-car fleet, as explained by the authors?

Mix together surging gasoline prices, a conflict in the Middle East, and a presidential election year [2004] and what do you get? Given the sorry state of economic education among our political elites, you are likely to find bad energy-policy proposals and an increased willingness to intervene in the very market forces that are necessary to promote trade, peace, and wealth creation.

Calls to Raise CAFE Standards

This likelihood is exemplified in the recent calls for raising the Corporate Average Fuel Economy (CAFE) standards. These 1970s-era regulations require the average car produced by an automobile manufacturer to meet a prescribed fuel-efficiency target in terms of miles per gallon.

They have always been popular with the left. Presidential candidate John F. Kerry's web site calls for increasing "our fuel economy standards to 36 miles per gallon by 2015." An Episcopal Church Public Policy Network "White Paper" argues that the "biggest single step we can take to save oil and curb global warming is to raise [CAFE] standards for both cars and light trucks." Newspapers from the *Seattle Times* to the *Birmingham News* have editorialized this year [2004] in favor of raising CAFE standards.

This knee-jerk proposal becomes popular every time gas prices spike at the pump, and we couldn't disagree more. Not only would raising CAFE requirements restrict individual choice and weaken the property rights of manufacturers, but the costs to drivers almost certainly outweigh the benefits, on average. This means that the cure would be worse than the disease.

Prices Change Despite Standards

CAFE standards were raised significantly from 1975 to 1984, a period when we experienced much higher gasoline prices, in real terms, than we are experiencing now. In 1980, for example, the price of gasoline hit $1.50 per gallon in Blacksburg, Virginia. Adjusted for transportation-related inflation from February 1980 to February 2004, the current price per gallon of that gasoline would be approximately $2.98. People responded to that dramatic price increase by changing their behavior in ways that reduced the overall cost of driving: they carpooled more; they planned their shopping more carefully to reduce the number of driving trips taken; and they bought more fuel-efficient cars. Oh, and by the way, the federal government raised CAFE requirements.

The high price of gasoline not only motivated changes in driver behavior, which led to decreased demand for gasoline; it also stimulated substantial new oil exploration and development of new reserves. The combination of reduced demand and increased supply had a predictable, if not inevitable, effect on gasoline prices. Starting in the mid-1980s, gasoline prices started coming down . . . and down . . . and down. Just three years ago [2001], we were paying well under a dollar per gallon in many parts of the country.

Much more than CAFE regulations caused such a welcome fall in prices. In fact, the regulations themselves can have the unintended effect of increasing gasoline demand if they encourage drivers to spend additional time on the road in more fuel-efficient cars than they would in less fuel-efficient cars. If this effect results in no net change in gasoline consumption, then CAFE is inherently self-defeating in its stated purpose.

Driving More Miles

The more fuel-efficient automobiles become, the more people want to drive. Instead of promoting conservation, CAFE standards have resulted in more people driving longer distances, consuming more gasoline. . . . In fact, according to the U.S. Department of Transportation's Bureau of Transportation Statistics, Americans are driving more than twice as many miles as they did thirty years ago.

Center for Individual Freedom, February 21, 2001. www.cfif.org.

Despite this possibility, the price of gasoline tumbled in the 1990s because of market forces, not because of CAFE standards (which, after all, have been set at 27.5 miles per gallon for the new passenger car fleet since 1990). This result is hardly surprising. Price signals dispersed among millions of independent economic actors play a much more significant role in affecting gasoline prices than commands from a few bureaucrats holed up in Washington, D.C.

Such economic history suggests that gas prices have both risen and fallen *in spite of* CAFE standards. Indeed, there are compelling reasons to believe that such standards only intensify the recent increase in the real cost of driving for motorists. Technologically, automobile manufacturers can meet higher standards in two principal ways. They can improve engine processing of the fuel and reduce the weight of vehicles (since a gallon of gasoline can push a lighter vehicle farther than a heavier vehicle).

Lighter Automobiles

Automobile firms, which have paid over a half a billion dollars since 1983 in CAFE-related civil fines, have a strong incentive to implement some combination of these solutions.

Historically, they did so by lightening the vehicles, replacing steel with aluminum. Because steel construction offers more protection, lightening the vehicles dramatically increased the safety risk and financial costs of being in an accident. (A 2001 study done by the Transportation Research Board, an "independent adviser to the federal government," concluded that lighter and smaller cars were likely responsible for 1,300–2,600 additional highway deaths in 1993.)

In response to this unintended consequence of government intervention in the market, air bags were required in the new-car fleet, another costly result of CAFE because federal safety rules do not allow for air bags to be reused. "Add the cost of labor, more than $1,000 for each air bag, and even more for the sensors, and the result is a totaled car," writes Eric Evarts in the *Christian Science Monitor*. Insurance-premium inflation, anyone?

Harmful to Society

Two points should be remembered the next time we read about traffic deaths on our highways. First, the lighter and less safe fleet of cars, thanks to CAFE, distorts the automobile market by causing some individuals to keep older and heavier cars longer than they otherwise would, and by increasing the demand for sports-utility vehicles, which escape such regulations. In the absence of more stringent mileage standards, at least some of these individuals would gladly pay more for gasoline (per year) in order to drive less fuel-efficient, but safer cars. There simply is no defensible reason to deny those people the opportunity to make the relevant implicit tradeoffs themselves, rather than trusting that the supposed savings in gasoline prices would, in fact, exceed the benefit from safer vehicles.

Second, CAFE standards inevitably lead to significantly higher vehicle costs *and* higher risk costs with little evidence that they are responsible, by themselves, for lowering gasoline prices. This implies that the social costs of raising CAFE standards substantially exceed the social benefits.

As the saying goes, the road to hell is paved with good intentions. We'd like to see lower gasoline prices. Thanks to the laws of supply and demand, the existence of higher-than-average prices virtually guarantees that prices will come down. Raising CAFE standards hinders this process and puts us on a road we don't want to be driving.

> *"Hydrogen offers the opportunity to end petroleum dependence and virtually eliminate . . . greenhouse gas emissions."*

Transitioning to a Hydrogen Economy Can Reduce Oil Dependence

Douglas L. Faulkner

In the following viewpoint Douglas L. Faulkner insists that the development of hydrogen as a fuel source would reduce America's reliance on fossil fuels. Moreover, according to Faulkner, hydrogen does not pollute like oil does when burned. The U.S. government has committed substantial resources to the development of hydrogen as a fuel, says Faulkner, and is already seeing significant progress. He believes that with future research, the United States will make the transition to a hydrogen economy in the near future. Faulkner is the acting assistant secretary for energy efficiency and renewable energy for the U.S. Department of Energy.

As you read, consider the following questions:

1. According to the author, what accounts for two-thirds of oil use in the United States?

Douglas L. Faulkner, testimony before the U.S. House Subcommittee on Energy and Resources, Committee on Government Reform, Washington, DC, July 27, 2005.

2. As cited by Faulkner, how much has the Department of Energy invested in projects to address critical hydrogen challenges?

3. According to the author, at what cost-per-gallon-of-gasoline equivalent can hydrogen be produced?

Over two years ago, in his 2003 State of the Union address, President [George W.] Bush announced the Hydrogen Fuel Initiative to reverse America's growing dependence on foreign oil by developing the hydrogen technologies needed for commercially-viable fuel cells—a way to power cars, trucks, homes, and businesses that could also significantly reduce criteria pollutants and greenhouse gas emissions. Since the launch of the five-year, $1.2-billion research initiative, we have had many accomplishments on the path to taking hydrogen and fuel cell technologies from the laboratory to the showroom in 2020. . . .

The Need for Hydrogen Research

As a Nation, we must work to ensure that we have access to energy that does not require us to compromise our economic security or our environment. Hydrogen offers the opportunity to end petroleum dependence and virtually eliminate transportation-related criteria[1] and greenhouse gas emissions by addressing the root causes of these issues. Imported petroleum already supplies more than 55 percent of U.S. domestic needs and those imports are projected to increase to more than 68 percent by 2025 with business-as-usual. Transportation accounts for two-thirds of the oil use in the United States and vehicles contribute to the Nation's air quality problems and greenhouse gas emissions because they release criteria pollutants and carbon dioxide.

1. The Environmental Protection Agency monitors levels of six main air pollutants, called criteria pollutants.

Summary of Key Drivers Affecting Hydrogen Energy Development

Support
- National security and the need to reduce oil imports.
- Global climate change and the need to reduce greenhouse gas emissions and pollution.
- Global population and economic growth and the need for new clean energy supplies at affordable prices, as hydrogen is potentially available in virtually unlimited supplies.
- Air quality and the need to reduce emissions from vehicles and power plants.

Inhibit
- The inability to build and sustain national consensus on energy policy priorities.
- Lack of a hydrogen infrastructure and the substantial costs of building one.
- Lack of commercially available, low-cost hydrogen production, storage, and conversion devices, such as fuel cells.
- Hydrogen safety issues.

Both support and inhibit
- Rapid pace of technological change in hydrogen and competing energy sources and technologies.
- The current availability of relatively low-cost fossil fuels, along with the inevitable depletion of these resources.
- Simultaneous consumer preferences for both clean environment and affordable energy supplies.

SOURCE: U.S. Department of Energy, 2002.

At the G8 Summit[2] earlier this month [July 2005] President Bush reiterated his policy of promoting technological innovation, like the development of hydrogen and fuel cell technologies, to address climate change, reduce air pollution and improve energy security in the United States and throughout the world. The [U.S. Department of Energy's, or DOE's,] R&D

2. An annual economic and political summit meeting of the most influential industrialized nations, including Canada, France, Germany, Italy, Japan, the United Kingdom, the United States and Russia—the so-called G8 countries.

[research and development] in high-efficiency vehicle technologies, such as gasoline-electric hybrid vehicles, will help improve energy efficiency and reduce the growth of petroleum consumption in the nearer term....

But, in the longer term, higher efficiency alone will not reduce our petroleum consumption; we ultimately need a substitute to replace petroleum. Hydrogen and fuel cells, when combined, have the potential to provide domestically-based, virtually carbon- and pollution-free power for transportation.

Hydrogen can be produced from diverse domestic energy resources, which include fossil fuels, nuclear energy, biomass, solar, wind and other renewables. We have planned and are executing a balanced research portfolio for developing hydrogen production and delivery technologies....

In the transition to the hydrogen economy, the DOE recognizes that hydrogen will be produced by technologies that do not require a large, up-front investment in hydrogen delivery infrastructure. Instead, hydrogen can be produced at the refueling station by reforming natural gas and renewable fuels like ethanol utilizing existing delivery infrastructure. A fuel cell vehicle running on hydrogen produced from natural gas would produce 25 percent less net carbon emissions than a gasoline-electric hybrid vehicle and 50 percent less than conventional internal combustion engine vehicles on a wheel-to-wheel basis. However, natural gas is not a long-term strategy because of concerns of limited supply and the demands of other sectors. As vehicle market penetration increases and research targets for the diverse hydrogen production and delivery technologies are met, these will help establish the business case for industry investment in large-scale hydrogen production and delivery infrastructure....

Progress

The DOE has made significant progress in planning and setting the stage to achieve the research breakthroughs necessary for a future hydrogen economy. The DOE has competitively selected over $510 million in projects to address critical challenges such as hydrogen storage, fuel cell cost and durability, and hydrogen production and delivery cost. In addition, we have established a national "learning" demonstration and new projects in safety, codes and standards, and education. All of the multi-year projects discussed below were competitively selected and are subject to congressional appropriations. The continuum of research, from basic science to technology demonstration, will be closely coordinated.

- In May 2005, 70 new projects were selected at $64 million over three years to focus on fundamental science and to enable revolutionary breakthroughs in hydrogen production, storage and fuel cells. . . .

- Three Centers of Excellence and 15 Independent projects were initiated in Hydrogen Storage at $150 million over five years to develop the most promising low-pressure storage approaches. The Centers include 20 universities, 9 federal laboratories and eight industry partners, representing a concerted, multidisciplinary effort to address on-board vehicular hydrogen storage.

- To address fuel cell cost and durability, five new projects were initiated at $13 million over three years. . . .

- A total of 65 projects were awarded for applied research in hydrogen production and delivery, funded at $107 million over four years. These include hydrogen production from renewables, distributed natural gas, coal and nuclear energy.

- A national vehicle and infrastructure "learning demonstration" project, a six-year effort with $170 million in DOE funding, was launched to take research from the laboratory to the real world, critically measuring progress and providing feedback to our R&D efforts.

- Approximately $7 million over four years for hydrogen education development was awarded to serve the needs of multiple target audiences, including state and local government officials, safety and code officials and local communities where hydrogen demonstrations are located.

With these new competitively selected awards, the best scientists and engineers from around the Nation are actively engaged. The stage is now set for results.

Achievements

Our ongoing research has already led to important technical progress.

- As highlighted by Secretary [of energy Samuel W.] Bodman in earlier Congressional testimony, the high volume cost of automotive fuel cells was reduced from $275 per kilowatt to $200 per kilowatt in two years. . . .

- In hydrogen production, we have demonstrated our ability to produce hydrogen at a cost of $3.60 per gallon of gasoline equivalent at an integrated fueling station that generates both electricity and hydrogen. This is down from about $5.00 per gallon of gasoline equivalent prior to the initiative. . . .

More Progress Ahead

DOE is looking to the future as well. Just as we have already made progress, we plan to have significant progress [in 2006]. . . .

The Department of Energy welcomes the challenge and opportunity to play a vital role in this Nation's energy future and to help address our energy security challenges in such a fundamental way.

| "The hydrogen economy has serious, perhaps fatal shortcomings."

Transition to a Hydrogen Economy Cannot Reduce Oil Dependence

David Morris

A hydrogen economy is not the solution to America's reliance on nonrenewable fuels such as oil, maintains David Morris in the following viewpoint. Morris argues that hydrogen extraction requires the use of fossil fuels or nuclear energy. Thus, in his opinion, pursuit of a hydrogen economy will simply continue America's dependence on nonrenewable energy and waste money that could be used to research and implement technologies using renewables instead. In addition, Morris points out, producing hydrogen from fossil fuels will pollute the air. Morris is vice president of the Institute for Local Self-Reliance.

As you read, consider the following questions:

1. According to Morris, how much of the world's commercial hydrogen now comes from natural gas?
2. How long has it taken for the renewable energy industry to capture 1 percent of the transportation market, according to the author?

3. Why will a hydrogen economy increase pollution, in Morris's opinion?

When George [W.] Bush proposed a $1.7 billion program to promote hydrogen-fueled cars in the [2003] State of the Union Address, both sides of the aisle applauded. Almost everyone supports a hydrogen economy—conservatives and liberals, tree huggers and oil drillers. Such unanimity forecloses serious discussion. That's unfortunate. An aggressive pursuit of a hydrogen economy is wrongheaded and short-sighted.

Hydrogen Extraction

To understand why, we need to start with the basics. Hydrogen is the most abundant element on the planet. But it cannot be harvested directly. It must be extracted from another material. There is an upside to this and a downside. The upside is that a wide variety of materials contain hydrogen, which is one reason it has attracted such widespread support. Everyone has a dog in this fight.

Renewable energy is a very little dog. Environmentalists envision an energy economy where hydrogen comes from water, and the energy used to accomplish this comes from wind. Big dogs like the nuclear industry also foresee a water-based hydrogen economy, but with nuclear as the power source that electrolyzes water. *Nucleonics Week* boasts that nuclear power "is the only way to produce hydrogen on a large scale without contributing to greenhouse gas emissions."

For the fossil fuel industry, not surprisingly, hydrocarbons will provide most of our future hydrogen. They already have a significant head start. Almost 50 percent of the world's commercial hydrogen now comes from natural gas. Another 20 percent is derived from coal.

The automobile and oil companies are betting that petroleum will be the hydrogen source of the future. It was General

Storage and Transportation of Hydrogen

Storing hydrogen in a compact way is a tricky problem, to say the least. Elemental hydrogen has the lowest density of any material in the universe. Trying to cram it together is like trying to circumvent basic physics; it just doesn't work. Liquefying the hydrogen consumes about a third of the energy stored in the hydrogen, and still the energy density of the resulting liquid hydrogen is only about one fourth of that of gasoline!

Kuro5hin, February 25, 2004, www.kuro5hin.org.

Motors, after all, that coined the phrase "the hydrogen economy."

Bad for Renewable Energy Technology

What does all this mean? A hydrogen economy will not be a renewable energy economy. For the next 20–50 years hydrogen will overwhelmingly be derived from fossil fuels or with nuclear energy.

Consider that it has taken more than 30 years for the renewable energy industry to capture 1 percent of the transportation fuel market (ethanol) and 2 percent of the electricity market (wind, solar, biomass). Renewables are poised to rapidly expand their presence. A hydrogen economy would be a potentially debilitating diversion.

As the President's 2004 budget demonstrates, any new money for hydrogen will be taken largely from budgets for energy efficiency and renewable energy. From a federal point of view, then, the more aggressively we pursue hydrogen, the less aggressively we pursue more beneficial technologies.

To be successful, a hydrogen initiative will require the expenditure of hundreds of billions of dollars to build an entirely new energy infrastructure (pipelines, fueling stations, automobile engines). Much of this will come from public money. Little of this expenditure will directly benefit renewables. Indeed, it is likely that renewable energy will have about the same share of the hydrogen market in 2040 as it now has of the transportation and electricity markets.

Far better to spend the billions the President wants to spend on hydrogen to increase renewable energy's share of the energy market from 1–2 percent to 25, 35, or even 50 percent in the same time frame.

Increasing Pollution

Not only will a hydrogen economy do little to expand renewable energy, it will increase pollution. Making hydrogen takes energy. We are using a fuel that could be used directly to provide electricity or mechanical power or heat to instead make hydrogen, which is then used to make electricity. Back in 1993 William Hoagland, senior project coordinator at the National Renewable Energy Laboratory's hydrogen program, prophetically told *Time Magazine*, "I can't see why anyone would invest in additional equipment to make hydrogen rather than simply putting the electricity on the grid."

We can, for example, run vehicles on natural gas or generate electricity using natural gas right now. Converting natural gas into hydrogen and then hydrogen into electricity increases the amount of greenhouse gases emitted.

Difficult to Transport and Store

There is another energy-related problem with hydrogen. It is the lightest element, about eight times lighter than methane. Compacting it for storage or transport is expensive and energy intensive. A recent study by two Swiss engineers concludes, "We have to accept that [hydrogen's] . . . physical properties are incompatible with the requirements of the energy market. Production, packaging, storage, transfer and delivery of the gas . . . are so energy consuming that alternatives should be considered."

The most compelling rationale for making hydrogen is that it is a way to store energy. That could benefit renewable energy sources like wind and sunlight that can't generate energy on demand. But batteries and flywheels can store electricity directly. The all-electric vehicle has not yet found a commercial market, but we should acknowledge the rapid advances made in electric storage technologies in the last few years.

Many people see the new hybrid vehicles as a bridge to a new type of transportation system. I agree, but with a different twist. Toyota and Honda are selling tens of thousands of cars that have small gas engines and batteries. American automobile companies will soon join them. Toyota and Honda and others are looking in the future to substitute a hydrogen fuel cell for the gasoline engine. That work should continue, but policymakers should also develop incentives and regulations that channel engineering ingenuity into improving the electric storage side of the hybrid system.

Currently, a Toyota Prius may get 5 percent of its overall energy from its batteries and could only go a mile or so as a zero emissions vehicle. A second-generation Prius might get 10 percent of its energy from batteries and might have a range of 2–3 miles. Why not encourage Toyota and Honda and others to increase the proportion of the energy they use from the batteries?

Fatal Shortcomings

We need to get beyond the glib, "we can run our cars on water," news bites and soberly assess the value of a massive national effort to convert to a hydrogen economy. When we do so, I believe, we will conclude that the hydrogen economy has serious, perhaps fatal shortcomings.

> "[The energy bill aims] to reduce our dependence on foreign oil, increase our domestic supply of energy, enhance energy efficiency, and strengthen our nation's energy infrastructure."

The 2005 Energy Bill Will Help Solve America's Energy Problems

Samuel Bodman

The following viewpoint is excerpted from Ask the White House, an online interactive forum where members of the public submit questions to administration officials. Samuel Bodman, the U.S. secretary of energy, explains that the 2005 energy bill will enhance America's energy infrastructure, increase energy supplies, and help reduce America's dependence on foreign oil. The bill does this by promoting energy conservation and the use of renewable fuels, says Bodman. Bodman, a former deputy secretary of the treasury, was appointed the eleventh secretary of energy in February 2005.

As you read, consider the following questions:

1. Why will daylight savings time be changed in March 2007, as explained by the author?

2. According to Bodman, why is U.S. energy cooperation with China important?

Samuel Bodman, "Ask the White House," www.whitehouse.gov, August 8, 2005.

3. How will the United States move away from a petroleum-based transportation sector, in the author's opinion?

Samuel Bodman: I was honored to be with President [George W.] Bush in New Mexico today [August 8, 2005] as he signed the nation's first comprehensive energy legislation in more than a decade. Four years ago, the President called upon Congress to craft a bill that would aim to reduce our dependence on foreign oil, increase our domestic supply of energy, enhance energy efficiency, and strengthen our nation's energy infrastructure. After much hard work and negotiation, the House and Senate recently passed an energy bill with broad bipartisan support. Today, with the President's signature, this legislation becomes law. . . .

The 2005 Energy Bill

Cliff, from Brimfield, Ohio, writes:

Secretary Bodman, in brief what are some of the short term parts of the Energy Bill and the long term parts? What kind of time frame are we talking [about]? . . .

Samuel Bodman: Thanks. This is a good question to kick things off. There are many measures in the bill for increasing America's energy security, but unfortunately there are no "quick fixes" to the energy challenges before us, as much as I wish there were. There are parts of the bill that will come on-line in the next few months, including tax credits for consumers who install energy-saving windows and insulation, solar-powered water heaters, or energy efficient air conditioners or furnaces in their homes; as well as tax credits for consumers who purchase hybrid gasoline-electric cars. . . .

In the medium time range, the bill promotes the greater use of renewable fuels such as ethanol and biodiesel, which we expect can play a part in reducing our dependence on imported petroleum.

Further down the road, the bill stimulates the development of new technology to generate clean, affordable energy. These technologies include clean coal plants, hydrogen fuel cells, and safe, emissions-free nuclear power.

Joshua, from Washington, D.C., writes:

Why are we changing the months for day light savings time? . . .

Samuel Bodman: Good question, Joshua. The provision in the energy bill to add an extra month to daylight savings time—three weeks in March, an extra one in November—was included at the behest of Congress. Supporters have claimed the extra hour of sunshine will dramatically cut down on oil consumption. Our Administration was concerned that the change might cause confusion in a variety of industries, such as the aviation, trucking and software industries. The newly extended daylight savings time goes into effect in March 2007, and we will be working to ensure that when the extension goes into effect, there won't be any unintended consequences.

Cooperating with China

Ionghua, from Chongqing, writes:

What is the policy about energy cooperation with [the People's Republic of China]?

Samuel Bodman: China and the U.S. both face very similar challenges with respect to energy in the coming decades. Our economies are expected to continue growing, and that means a growing demand for energy. Moreover, we also share concerns about the environmental effects of energy use. Because of these various shared energy challenges, the Department of Energy has reached out to the Chinese government on ways we can work together to solve our energy problems. We recently hosted Chinese government and industry officials at our Department as part of the U.S.-China Energy Policy Dialogue. Discussions ranged from sharing energy efficiency technology to next-generation nuclear power know-how to clean-coal technology. We are confident that by communicating information, sharing research, and pooling resources, our two nations can benefit in ways that each one, acting alone, could not.

Solar Power

Michael, from Powell, TN, writes:

Have we considered using solar power?

Samuel Bodman: We've done more than consider it. Solar is an important part of our overall emphasis on increasing the use of renewable energy sources, including wind, hydro, and biomass energy. To generate large amounts of cost-effective electricity from solar energy, we need to improve technology for solar cells, and the Department of Energy [DOE] is making a significant investment in that. This is something that I personally am quite enthusiastic about. Not long ago I visited a solar cell manufacturing facility in Michigan, run by a company called Uni-Solar. In partnership with DOE, this company and others are really pushing the envelope to make solar energy technology serve a greater portion of our energy needs.

Also, as I mentioned, the energy bill signed by the President, contains important tax incentives for homeowners to make greater use of solar power, including up to $2,000 for the installation of solar-powered hot-water systems.

Addressing High Gas Prices

Ryan, from New Hampshire, writes:

Hello Mr. Bodman, I was just wondering when the gas prices will go down? Also, I heard Mr. President talking about the oil in Alaska that we will use. When would that be finished? On that same day I also heard him say that we will be building a new nuclear hydrogen power plant. . . . When will those be done? . . .

Samuel Bodman: Unfortunately, Ryan, there is no magic bullet that will bring down gasoline prices. President Bush is

Encouraging Conservation and Energy Efficiency

The Energy Bill:

- Establishes new energy efficiency standards for a wide variety of consumer products and commercial appliances, and offers tax incentives to encourage their purchase

- Encourages improved efficiency in homes and buildings, establishes new aggressive Federal energy savings goals, and reauthorizes the Energy Savings Performance Contract program to conserve more energy at Federal facilities

- Offers tax incentives to consumers to purchase energy efficient hybrid, clean diesel, and fuel cell vehicles

- Requires a new, multi-year rulemaking by the Department of Transportation to increase fuel economy standards for passenger cars, light trucks, and SUVs [sport utility vehicles].

White House, July 29, 2005, www.whitehouse.gov.

concerned about the impact of high gas prices for working Americans, and let me assure you that if the President had a magic wand that could lower prices, he would do it! The high prices we've been experiencing have been symptoms of our country's larger energy problems. These problems—from inadequate infrastructure and refining capacity to a regulatory structure that has discouraged needed investment—have been a long time in the making. They will take some time to get sorted out. And while the Energy bill that President Bush signed today can't bring the price you pay at the pump down overnight, it puts us on a path to address the underlying problems that confront our energy sector.

As for Alaskan oil, I assume you are referring to the oil in the Arctic National Wildlife Refuge, or ANWR. The Bush Administration supports the idea of opening a limited area of ANWR to environmentally responsible oil exploration. This issue, however, was not part of the comprehensive energy bill President Bush signed today, though we expect Congress to take it up in the coming months. Assuming Congress acts (and bipartisan majorities in both houses appear to support opening ANWR), it would still be several years before large-scale production could occur.

Finally, the President has made a big push for the resurgence of nuclear power—which is the only energy source we currently have that can produce large quantities of electricity with no air pollution or greenhouse gas emissions. Yet no nuclear power plant has been built in the U.S. in several decades. If we are going to meet our economy's growing need for electricity, however, we are going to need nuclear power to play a big role. That is why we worked with Congress for critical energy bill provisions to support our stated goal of constructing new nuclear power plants. . . .

Reducing Petroleum Dependence

James, from El Paso, Texas, writes:

Mr. Secretary, hydrogen fuel cells are the energy source of the future. What criteria are being used to select wisely researchers to move us forward in this direction? . . .

Samuel Bodman: The President announced a very ambitious hydrogen fuel cell research program in his 2003 State of the Union address to Congress. Since then we have moved forward with a large-scale international consortium called the International Partnership for the Hydrogen Economy [IPHE]. This group of 16 countries and the European Commission is working in cooperation on research for fuel cell high-temperature membranes, hydrogen storage materials, and renewable energy production. The IPHE allows all the nations interested in hydrogen to pool resources, to have our scientists and engineers share knowledge, and to lay important pre-competitive groundwork, like developing interoperable codes and standards.

Kathy, from Seattle, writes:

Despite oil prices at record highs, our oil companies are producing less oil this year than last, with some major oil companies producing less oil each year for years now. Does the energy bill do enough to reduce our dependence on oil, and will we be able to avoid an energy crisis?

Samuel Bodman: Moving away from a petroleum-based transportation sector—and thus dramatically reducing our dependence on imported energy—is one of President Bush's most important energy goals. We are very committed to moving the United States into the hydrogen economy. In addition to the international efforts I just mentioned, our Department is working aggressively to implement the President's Hydrogen Fuel Initiative, a $1.2 billion commitment to move hydrogen fuel cell technology from the laboratory to the showroom.

John, from Texas, writes:

Is it true we're going to run out of oil in 50 years?

Samuel Bodman: While the world still has plenty of oil, it's a fact that fossil fuels are finite resources that will not last forever. And while we are not in danger of running out in the near term, oil is becoming more difficult to find and produce, especially as demand for energy continues to climb. That is why energy diversity is a key element of the President's National Energy Policy. We need a variety of energy sources as well as suppliers. These diverse sources include hydrogen, as I just mentioned, as well as biofuels and ethanol for transportation. And for the long-term, we also are looking at the potential of sources like nuclear fusion.

| "Neither energy security nor national security are improved by the Energy Policy Act of 2005."

The 2005 Energy Bill Will Not Solve America's Energy Problems

Sarasota Herald Tribune

In the following viewpoint the Sarasota Herald Tribune, *a daily Florida newspaper, argues that the 2005 energy bill is not an effective solution to the energy problems faced by the United States. America must reduce its dependence on foreign oil, maintains the* Tribune, *which could be achieved by encouraging fuel economy and conservation. However, according to the newspaper, the 2005 bill requires neither. Instead, says the* Tribune, *the bill focuses on exploiting domestic oil supplies, which are finite.*

As you read, consider the following questions:

1. What has President Bush promised since 2001, according to the *Tribune*?

2. As cited by the author, how much of America's oil will the nation have to import in 2025?

3. According to the *Tribune*, what consumes 40 percent of the oil America uses?

Moments before the Senate voted to pass an energy bill that does little to lessen the nation's dangerous dependence on oil, the legislation's chief sponsor ended the floor debate with a defensive whimper aimed at opponents.

"You cannot order Americans to buy little tiny cars," Republican Sen. Pete Domenici of New Mexico said Friday.

Domenici was giving his explanation of why the Energy Policy Act of 2005 doesn't require U.S. manufacturers of cars and trucks to improve fuel efficiency.

What he did not explain is why the mammoth legislation—the first overhaul of energy policy in 13 years—does so little to encourage fuel economy and conservation.

Dependence on Foreign Oil

Since 2001, President [George W.] Bush has promised Americans an energy policy that would lessen dependence on foreign oil. But the energy bill—which the House earlier approved and which the president says he will sign[1]—doesn't do that.

"We'll be dependent on the global market for more than half our oil for as long as we're using oil, and the energy bill isn't going to change that," Ben Lieberman of the Heritage Foundation told the *Washington Post*.

Fifty-eight percent of the oil used in the United States is imported, analysts told the *Post*, and U.S. officials estimate that the nation will have to import 68 percent in 2025. At best, the analysts say, provisions in the bill would slightly slow the growth in the demand for foreign oil.

The concern about foreign oil stems from the fact that much of it comes from the politically unstable Middle East. If imports from that region are reduced, the oil-dependent U.S. economy would suffer.

1. The bill was signed on August 8, 2005.

Tax Breaks for the Oil Industry

The energy bill that passed the House on July 28, 2005 and the Senate on July 29, 2005 includes at least $4 billion in subsidies and tax breaks for the oil industry. At the same time, this new energy law allows Big Oil to plunder the federal treasury by paying even less in taxes and royalties for publicly-owned resources. The final energy policy also weakens environmental protections while doing nothing to reduce America's dependence on oil or relieve consumers at the pump.

Alan Simpson, E2M Energy Newsroom, 2005. www.energy2m.com.

Yet, the president and Congress have failed to acknowledge that oil—whether foreign or domestic—is a finite, increasingly expensive and environmentally damaging source of energy.

Exploiting Domestic Oil

The energy bill puts too little emphasis on developing sustainable energy sources and too much attention on exploiting domestic oil. For example:

- A planned oil and gas inventory will include the ecologically fragile eastern Gulf of Mexico in what could be the first step toward drilling off Florida's coast.

- Oil, gas, coal and utility companies get most of the billions of dollars in tax breaks that the new bill dishes out.

- And, of course, U.S. automakers aren't required to improve gas mileage.

Fuel Economy Must Be Addressed

"The single biggest step that Congress could take to reduce our oil dependency is to significantly increase the fuel economy standards of cars and trucks that Americans drive," Kevin Knobloch, president of the Union of Concerned Scientists, told the *Post*.

Cars and light trucks consume 40 percent of the oil America uses, and light trucks—a category that includes pickups, sport utility vehicles [SUVs], vans, and minivans—account for half of this, according to the group Environmental Defense.

"Simply requiring SUVs and other light trucks to improve their fuel economy by 1 mile per gallon per year could save more than 1.5 million barrels of oil per day by 2020, about as much oil as we currently import from Saudi Arabia," the group said in a recent news release.

The U.S. Environmental Protection Agency [EPA] acknowledged the strategic importance of energy efficiency in an annual report initially scheduled for release [in July 2005] stating that "fuel economy is directly related to energy security." A copy of the report was sent to *The New York Times* before EPA officials decided to delay its release amid Congress' debate of the energy bill.

As Domenici says, Congress cannot force Americans to buy smaller, more fuel-efficient cars. But Congress has a responsibility to craft an energy policy that protects not only the country's long-term economic security but also, in this era of global political unrest, the national security.

Neither energy security nor national security are improved by the Energy Policy Act of 2005.

Periodical Bibliography

The following articles have been selected to supplement the diverse views presented in this chapter.

Mark Baard — "Hydrogen's Dirty Details," *Village Voice*, January 7–13, 2004.

Congressional Digest — "Americans and Their Cars: The Debate over Fuel Economy Standards," May 2002.

Issues and Controversies On File — "Gasoline Taxes," June 25, 2004.

Amory Lovins — "How America Can Free Itself of Oil—Profitably," *Fortune*, October 2004.

Robert Olson — "The Promise and Pitfalls of Hydrogen Energy," *Futurist*, July/August 2003.

Michael Parfit — "After Oil: Powering the Future," *National Geographic*, August 2005.

Charley Reese — "The Myth of Independence," *Conservative Chronicle*, June 23, 2004.

Regulation — "CAFE Standards," Spring 2004.

Linda Rowan — "The Energy Bill: Is It Big and Broad Enough? *Geotimes*, July 2005.

Jerry Taylor and Peter Van Doren — "High-Octane Amnesia," *Wall Street Journal*, April 12, 2005.

Nicholas Varchaver — "How to Kick the Oil Habit," *Fortune*, August 23, 2004.

Matthew L. Wald — "Wind Power Is Becoming a Better Bargain," *New York Times*, February 13, 2005.

Caspar W. Weinberger — "An Energy Bill—at Last," *Forbes*, October 3, 2005.

OPPOSING
VIEWPOINTS®
SERIES

How Does Oil Impact International Relations?

Chapter Preface

Suzhou, located in eastern China, is one of that country's oldest cities, with centuries-old villages, cobblestone streets, and picturesque canals. While the city showcases China's long history, however, it also epitomizes the rapid development that characterizes China today—development that is dramatically increasing China's consumption of oil. Five years ago, there were 30,000 cars in Suzhou. Today there are 150,000, with an additional 150 being sold every day. Such growth in car ownership and other signs of increasing economic prosperity have resulted in the nation's consuming an increasing proportion of the world's oil. Examining how China's growing need for energy is impacting the globe provides insight into how oil affects international relations.

Other nations that import oil are concerned that as China's consumption of oil grows, worldwide oil supplies will be strained. China predicts that the number of cars and trucks on its roads will increase sevenfold, to 140 million by 2020. The U.S. Energy Information Administration (EIA) believes that as a result of new cars flooding China's roads, through 2025 the country's oil consumption will increase two and a half times as fast per year as the average for industrialized Western nations. Journalist Ronald Brownstein warns that this "enormous increase in [China's] consumption of fossil fuels" is likely to raise world oil prices. His supposition is based on the economic theory that says that when demand rises, so do prices. He adds, "The direct result for the United States and other nations could be . . . higher prices at the pump." Michael R. Wessel of the U.S.-China Economic and Security Review Commission agrees. "The higher their demand, the higher oil . . . prices are going to go up," he says. "The China problem is here to stay."

Many people worry that China's rising demand for oil will cause more international competition. Journalist Jehangir Pocha explains that China is currently taking steps to secure access to the oil it will need in the future. She says, "China, which has already invested about $15 billion in foreign oil fields, is expected to spend 10 times more over the next decade." According to researcher Bill Powell, China's actions may affect other nations' access to oil. "Competitors are worried that China is so eager to do deals that it will warp the market," he says. "Western oil consumers are concerned that 'they won't be able to compete.'" It is widely believed that such competition will be a major factor influencing international relations in the future. As author Paul Roberts argues, "It seems more and more likely that the race for a piece of the last big reserves of oil and natural gas will be the dominant geopolitical theme of the 21st century."

Some concerned analysts compare China's economic development to America's development history. They point out that China appears to be following in America's development path, but warn that world oil supplies may not be able to support China's growth. The United States currently consumes approximately one quarter of the world's oil. While China has a far larger population than does the United States—more than 1 billion versus almost 300 million, respectively—it has historically consumed far less energy. According to the EIA, China consumed only 40 percent as much energy as the United States in 2005. However, as China's economy grows, analysts realize these percentages will change. According to Rick Schulberg, director of the China-U.S. Center for Sustainable Development, "China's economic development is so rapid that it is taking just forty years to achieve what took the United States one hundred and fifty." There is widespread fear that if China begins to demand as much oil per person as the United States does, world oil supplies will quickly be depleted.

As the following chapter reveals, China's oil consumption is only one of the factors affecting global interactions. With oil so vital to national economies, the question of how oil impacts international relations will likely remain central to debates about this limited resource.

"In the Gulf states especially, there is a near-universal view . . . that the fundamental element [in the Iraq war] . . . is oil."

U.S. Involvement in the 2003 Iraq War Was Motivated by Oil

Paul Rogers

In the following viewpoint Paul Rogers asserts that the United States did not start a war in Iraq in 2003 in order to help spread democracy in the Middle East. Instead, says Rogers, the war was motivated by America's desire to control oil supplies in Iraq. He backs up his claim by pointing out that the Middle East contains much of the world's oil and that the United States is deeply dependent upon foreign sources of oil to fuel its economy. Rogers is professor of peace studies at Bradford University in the United Kingdom and the international security editor for openDemocracy, *an online magazine of global politics and culture.*

As you read, consider the following questions:

1. According to the author, how has the Bush administration treated the number of deaths and injuries in Iraq?

2. How much of the world's oil is located in the Gulf region, according to Rogers?

3. As argued by the author, with which two countries is the
   United States engaged in competition for the world's oil
   resources?

The Iraq war launched by a United States-led coalition [in
March 2003], is still [in 2005] causing intense embarrass-
ment to its two main protagonists. In Britain, there is continuing controversy over the legal advice given to Tony Blair's
administration on the eve of war by the government's senior
legal officer, the attorney-general. In the United States, Washington politicians and commentators point to the Iraqi elec-
tions and a decrease in insurgent activity as evidence for opti-
mism, but these cannot conceal the enormous human and
financial costs of the war, especially at a local level.

A Costly War

In two years of war and insurgency, over 1,500 US troops have
been killed and 11,500 injured, and many thousands more re-
turned to the homeland because of accidental injury, physical
or mental illness. Even in the context of a slight post-election
decrease in the pitch of the insurgency, 222 troops were injured in the first three weeks of March [2005], 82 of them seriously.

The Bush administration has been assiduous in downplay-
ing these deaths and injuries, and the national media rarely
pays much attention (a few papers, such as the *Washington
Post*, are notable exceptions). At the same time, local newspapers across the United States do cover the intimate stories of
young men returning in coffins or having slowly to recover
from serious injuries.

Historical Revision

The official US view about the war's justification remains
firm: that [former Iraqi president] Saddam Hussein was an increasing threat, that his overthrow has brought democracy to

Iraq, and that the regional consequences of the war across the region are positive. This perspective conveniently downplays other elements of the historical record, such as US support for Saddam Hussein against Iran during the Iran-Iraq war [1980–1988] and his most brutal assaults against the Kurds.[1] In 1988, for example, the US Navy's destruction of most of the modern facilities of the small Iranian navy in the Persian Gulf occurred close to Saddam's *Anfal* campaigns against the Kurds in northern Iraq.

The argument that the war has helped spread democracy across the Middle East equally involves a revision of the historical record. Donald Rumsfeld, US secretary of defense, ... stated that the Iraq war would have been much easier for the United States if Turkey had allowed military access to US forces; but the refusal was decided by the elected Turkish parliament. Indeed, there is endemic suspicion in the Middle East that if a cluster of states there really did embrace fully democratic processes that were free of US pressure, its electors' choice would be demands for wholesale US withdrawal from the region and a cessation of its support for Israel.

The Black Gold Hunger

The most important factor that illuminates the contrast between rhetoric and reality over the war, however, is one that is discussed in the Middle East far more often than in the United States and Britain. In the Gulf states especially, there is a near-universal view among academics and policy analysts that the fundamental element in the developments of the past three years, far more important even than the US commitment to Israel, is oil.

When [former U.S. president] Bill Clinton was campaigning for the White House, his advisors were so convinced that

---

1. This ethnic group was severely oppressed under Saddam. In 1988 he killed thousands of Kurds with chemical weapons, and some people charge that the United States responded by trying to shift the blame to Iran.

Oil Means Power

There is plenty of circumstantial evidence mounting that the real reason for the American invasion of Iraq was the most obvious one: Oil. In this case, "oil" doesn't mean that we went to war for the commercial benefit of U.S. oil companies—and in fact, as I reported in *Mother Jones* magazine in early 2003, before the war, most U.S. oil firms and their executives were against the war. But in Iraq, "oil" means the strategic commodity that is the single most important world resource. Even a novice geostrategist knows that who controls oil controls the world. And in this case, America's rival for control of oil is, first and foremost, China.

Robert Dreyfuss, July 18, 2005. www.tompaine.com.

the election would be won or lost on "pocket-book" issues that they prominently displayed a slogan on the campaign-room wall: "It's the economy, stupid!" Substitute "oil" for "economy" and this is the view that echoes increasingly loudly the further you travel from Washington and the closer you get to the Gulf states.

It is both striking and curious that this view contrasts so strongly with those of many Western analysts, although this may be starting slowly to change. But if the "oil factor" does move closer to the centre of political discussion in the West, two different aspects of it, short-term and long-term, must be distinguished in order to understand what really motivates US policy in the region.

A strong argument proposed by anti-war voices in 2002–03 was that the war's purpose was to allow US oil companies to seize Iraqi oil fields and reap huge rewards in the process. The huge lobbying power of transnational oil companies in search of short-term gain or "plunder" was seen as a key motivator of US strategy.

Whether or not direct lobbying had an effect, the result of the Iraq war has certainly been "good" for the oil industry. Oil-related companies like Halliburton have found Iraq immensely profitable, and the oil companies themselves are currently enjoying exceptional profitability.

At the same time, the oil companies' financial successes relate only indirectly to Iraq and follow a pattern well-known during the 1973–74 and 1989–90 oil price surges. In any period of suddenly rising oil prices, the big transnational companies are adept at quickly passing price increases to consumers. The practice is to transfer "well-head" price increases to consumers within, at the most, a month of those increases taking effect. The companies have perhaps a hundred days of supply at the old prices as the black gold gushes through the complex system of tank farms, oil-tankers plying the sea routes, refineries and final distribution; profit-taking from sales while prices remain high is the order of the day.

Such "bull" market conditions—periods of rising pricing when the market is expanding—are almost always good for resource industries. But the key issue in the Gulf region is not cyclical but structural: a long-term trend towards the progressively greater reliance of the world economy on Gulf oil. This is measured in terms of decades, not months.

Increasing Competition for Oil

The Gulf region has nearly two-thirds of all the world's known oil reserves, and more keeps getting found—in contrast to oil fields in the United States, the North Sea and elsewhere that are in decline. Moreover, Gulf oil is high quality, easy to extract and very cheap, much more so even than the far smaller reserves of the Caspian basin. In the short term, intense exploitation of reserves in Africa and central America, coupled with drilling in Alaska, may ease US import demands, but the long-term trend is all in favour of the Gulf.

Moreover, it is not just the United States that needs the oil—Europe, China, the east Asian "tiger economies" and increasingly India are huge oil importers; they will require even greater resources from the Gulf as it becomes *the* key oil-exporting region of the world. This kind of thinking has prompted Iran's recent long-term deals with China and India[2] and makes these countries (along with Japan) deeply concerned over their increasing energy dependence on Gulf oil.

Motivated by Oil

This kind of assessment suggests that any talk of US commitment to democracy is peripheral, and only relevant if it ensures increasing US influence, backed by powerful military forces. In short, Washington is seen as engaged in a long-term process of indirect control of the region, at a time of intense competition with China and India for leverage over the world's oil resources. In turn this is crucial to the future of the "new American century".

Perhaps, by the end of this decade, the view that the Iraq war of 2003 was essentially motivated by oil will become routine among Western analysts—and the fact that it was close to academic heresy at the time of the war forgotten. If so, it will be a case of the West's opinion-formers catching up with views embedded in the Middle East, whose own experts have long since recognised that this indeed is the "great game" of the early 21st century.

---

2. In 2004 China signed a $70 billion natural gas import deal with Iran.

| *"As a business decision, invading Iraq
'for the oil' is a loser, a big loser."*

U.S. Involvement in the 2003 Iraq War Was Not Motivated by Oil

Charles A. Kohlhaas

The following viewpoint is excerpted from an article written by Charles A. Kohlhaas two weeks prior to the 2003 invasion of Iraq. Kohlhaas argues that the imminent invasion is not motivated by America's desire for oil. In his opinion, common sense shows that invading Iraq would be an extremely bad business decision that would not yield any oil profits for the United States. He predicts that such an invasion will actually lead to a reduction in Iraqi oil production. Kohlhaas is a former professor of petroleum engineering at the Colorado School of Mines and has worked for numerous companies in the international oil and gas industry.

As you read, consider the following questions:

1. Why must the United States consider the cost of an invasion of Iraq, as argued by Kohlhaas?

2. According to the author, what would be the cost of developing oil fields elsewhere to replace Iraqi production?

3. Why is the development of new Iraqi oil fields likely to take a long time, in Kohlhaas's opinion?

Nothing demonstrates the political and moral bankruptcy of the American liberal left more clearly than the current attempt to portray military action against Iraq as "for the oil". At first this seemed to be only a claim by the usual suspects that quickly moved onto certain editorial pages. But it entered the Presidential campaign with Congressman Dennis Kucinich's preposterous claim on [the weekly television program] "Meet the Press" that Iraq contains *five trillion dollars' worth of oil*, syllogistically followed by the allegation that such an amount of oil is the obvious reason for an invasion. The allegation was countered on the program forcefully by [political adviser] Richard Perle, but we can expect to hear it again. Not only is the allegation base, but the logic is flawed and the numbers are wrong.

How Congressman Kucinich could come up with 5 trillion dollars for the value of oil in Iraq is a mystery. The flagrant misrepresentation in this assertion seems to be an attempt to trivialize an invasion as motivated by a business decision on behalf of one of the left's favorite scapegoats—the oil business. Such a characterization fails on the basis of being an extremely bad business decision.

Cost-Benefit Analysis

All wars are fought for economic reasons if staying alive and not being enslaved are included as economic benefits even though difficult to quantify in dollars and cents. An invasion "for the oil", however, implies an objective which is tangible, quantifiable and has a price posted on a daily basis. A war "for the oil" thus can be subjected to a cost-benefit analysis.

Iraq produces a bit more than 2 million barrels of oil per day (bopd) now [in March 2003]. . . .

The most common concern regarding the possible effect of an invasion on oil production is that oil operations will be disrupted during military action. Disruption probably will reduce world supplies and drive oil prices up on the world markets for a short-term. A less probable, but nevertheless real, concern is that [Iraqi leader Saddam Hussein] will sabotage or contaminate the fields and cause supply disruptions and higher prices for a medium to long-term.[1] So the most likely outcome of an Iraqi invasion is a reduction of supplies and increased prices; clearly an additional cost attributable to an invasion, not a benefit, and exactly contrary to a claim that the invasion is "for the oil".

If we consider a post-invasion situation in which the disruptions and price effects of the invasion have passed and damage to the fields has somehow been prevented, Iraq would again be producing at about its current rate. It produces at that rate now. Where is the gain?[2]

Not a Profitable Decision

Estimates of the costs to the government of the United States for an invasion of Iraq seem to be mostly between $50 billion to $200 billion. If we invade Iraq for oil, the U.S. government must be able to derive a benefit from the oil greater than this cost. What is not clear is how Washington would be paid back for the war. . . .

Investment required to find and develop oil supplies is generally in the range of $10,000 to $15,000 per daily barrel of production in the United States and $5000 to $12,000 internationally. Some production can be developed in Saudi Arabia for as low as $3000, but foreign companies are not allowed to operate in Saudi Arabia. For a total investment probably between $10 billion and $20 billion, supplies can be developed elsewhere to replace the 2 million bopd of Iraqi production;

1. This did not happen.

2. As of this writing more than two years after the invasion of Iraq, oil production was at lower levels than before the war. This was primarily the result of continuing military conflict there, which hampers production.

Blood for Oil?

If the argument is that war is primarily being executed to ensure global access to Iraqi oil reserves, then it flounders upon misunderstanding. The only thing preventing Iraqi oil from entering the world market in force [in 2003] is the partial U.N. embargo on Iraqi exports. Surely if access to Iraqi oil were the issue, it would have occurred to [President George W.] Bush and [British prime minister Tony] Blair that removing the embargo is about $100 billion cheaper (and less risky politically) than going to war.

Jerry Taylor, Cato Institute, March 18, 2003. www.cato.org.

much cheaper than the cost of an invasion and without the risks and unpleasant aspects of military action.

Could we increase production in Iraq after an invasion? Yes, but that increase would also require investment just as it would anywhere. We can make that investment in Iraq if the opportunity is available or elsewhere if it is not. But in Iraq any investment for oil would be increased by the large sunk cost of the war. That cost is not justified by the amount of oil production. Nothing is changed by an invasion and the cost of the war is still a large cost without any return based on oil.

A Bad Business Decision

From a political and diplomatic standpoint, the United States will probably not be able to impose *any* taxes or fees on the production nor take any competitive advantage for American companies. . . . Immediate objectives will be to encourage formation of a stable government and political system. Control and administration of the oil industry will probably remain in the hands of Iraqis.[3]

3. As of this writing, the Iraqi oil industry was under the control of the Iraqi government.

First priority will be to rehabilitate the existing wells, fields, facilities, and infrastructure that are quite dilapidated after years of isolation from modern technology, services, and materials. Except for the costs of this rehabilitation, oil income will probably be used for general governmental purposes to rebuild the country and its infrastructure and services. Therefore, any expansion into development of new fields will probably require foreign capital and a significant increase of activity by foreign companies. Privatization of the fields is not a practical possibility, so foreign investment and activity will be in the form of contracts for which the operating, fiscal, procurement, labor, liability, insurance, accounting, legal and regulatory terms must be established. Such a process is subject to lengthy political and bureaucratic delays.

So not only can the United States not receive any direct payback of the cost of the war from the oil, but any significant increase of Iraqi supplies will probably not be realized for a few, or possibly several, years.

As a business decision, invading Iraq "for the oil" is a loser, a big loser. Anyone who would propose, in a corporate boardroom, invading Iraq for the oil would probably find his career rather short. No, the slogan "no war for oil" is a blatant misrepresentation propagated for political reasons.

"Like it or not, the maintenance of Saudi Arabia as a supplier of last resort is . . . necessary."

The United States Cannot Escape Dependence on Saudi Arabian Oil

Joe Barnes, Amy Jaffe, and Edward L. Morse

In the following viewpoint Joe Barnes, Amy Jaffe, and Edward L. Morse argue that while U.S. dependence on Saudi Arabian oil is undesirable, it is inescapable. While Russia, Iraq, Africa, and South America are alternative sources of oil, they are not reliable, due to political and technical problems, argue the authors. In their opinion, the United States will be forced to continue relying on oil from Saudi Arabia. The authors note that such reliance could result in America becoming even more vulnerable to terrorists, who are supported by Saudi Arabia. Barnes is a research fellow at the Baker Institute for Public Policy at Rice University in Houston, Texas; Jaffe is the Wallace Wilson Fellow for energy studies at the Baker Institute; and Morse is an executive adviser at Hess Energy Trading Company.

As you read, consider the following questions:

1. How do the authors define America's "special relationship" with Saudi Arabia?

Joe Barnes, Amy Jaffe, and Edward L. Morse, "The New Geopolitics of Oil," *The National Interest*, Winter 2003/2004, pp. 7–15. Copyright © 2003 by *The National Interest*. Reproduced by permission.

2. According to Barnes, Jaffe, and Morse what does Russia need in order to exploit reserves in its more remote areas?

3. With which country will the United States be competing for oil in Africa, as explained by the authors?

No one is satisfied with the current energy policy status quo; but few seem willing to make the hard decisions and uncomfortable compromises necessary to do anything about it. And no party has sole ownership of the status quo. It represents a continuation of the policy of successive administrations in Washington over the past quarter century in encouraging diversity of global oil production, cooperation with major oil producers—especially Saudi Arabia—to ensure stable markets, research in alternative fuels as a hedge against long-term price increases and reliance on a robust strategic petroleum reserve for use in cases of extreme market volatility. . . .

The "Special Relationship"

The centerpiece of the status quo is "the special relationship" with Saudi Arabia—a strategic *quid pro quo* under which the United States would guarantee the security of Saudi Arabia in return for Riyadh's cooperation in keeping a reliable flow of moderately priced oil to international petroleum markets. The first pillar of the special relationship is the decisive role that Saudi Arabia plays in international oil markets. Riyadh is not only the world's largest exporter of oil, but possesses a quarter of global petroleum reserves and, significantly, excess capacity for use in an emergency. The second pillar is the ability and willingness of the United States to intervene militarily should Saudi Arabia be threatened. Washington did so, most notably when it rushed troops to Saudi Arabia when Iraq invaded Kuwait in 1990.

The September 11 [2001 terrorist] attacks, however, renewed the impetus to reassess the U.S.-Saudi relationship. The fact that [terrorist leader] Osama bin Laden and 15 of 19 [of the September 11] suicide bombers were Saudi nationals lent the long-standing neoconservative critique of Saudi Arabia great public salience. Since 9/11, neoconservative commentators have stepped up their attacks on Saudi Arabia, openly branding the kingdom an "enemy," and have included Riyadh in the list of Middle East capitals—along with Tehran [Iran] and Damascus [Syria]—where "regime change" would be desirable. . . .

The Neoconservative Vision for Oil

So, are there alternatives to the unsatisfactory status quo? Some neoconservatives offer one: a radical shift of policy that would see Washington play an altogether more assertive role in the oil arena. Diversity of supply would not just be an economic end but a strategic means. The United States would attempt to drive down the price of oil, break the ability of OPEC [Organization of the Petroleum Exporting Countries] to set prices, and deprive unfriendly states—including Saudi Arabia—of revenue. The neoconservative approach resembles U.S. oil strategy during the Cold War, when during the Reagan Administration [1981–89], Washington encouraged Saudi Arabia to suppress prices in order to cause economic damage to the Soviet Union.

Neoconservative concerns (and increasingly left of center commentators as well) center on a belief that oil revenues permit countries like Libya, Iran and Saudi Arabia to sustain authoritarian regimes and promote anti-American policies. Collusion on production levels through OPEC, in turn, sustains those rents at a high level. Saudi Arabia, though nominally an ally of the United States, plays a particularly pernicious role under neoconservative ideology, by using its immense oil revenues and leadership in OPEC to promote the Kingdom's own brand of fundamentalist Islam—Wahhabism—in the Middle East and Central Asia.

At one level, the neoconservative argument is logical: low oil prices—in addition to providing substantial economic benefits for the United States and global economies—will reduce the revenue available to oil states, which sponsor terrorism or pursue the acquisition of weapons of mass destruction. But it both overestimates the ability of the United States to sustain low international oil prices and underestimates the consequences of a general decline in oil prices for oil producing allies of the United States. It assumes that the United States will be able to persuade major oil producers like Russia and a post-occupation Iraq to pursue policies against their own economic interests. . . .

Russia to the Rescue?

Reducing—if not ending—our reliance on Saudi Arabia requires cooperation with other major oil producers. Russia leads the list. Russian oil output has recovered sharply from its lows of 6 million barrels per day (bpd) in the mid-1990s. It reached 8.6 million bpd by mid-2003 and is expected to exceed 9 million bpd by the beginning of 2004.[1] Exports show an equally dramatic increase, now making Russia the largest non-OPEC exporter in the world, and second only to Saudi Arabia in total world exports. . . .

But Russia faces serious obstacles in its quest to equal, much less surpass, Saudi Arabia in international oil markets. Despite significant strides in recent years, the Russian business climate remains marked by inadequate rule of law protections. Standards of transparency, accountability and protection of minority shareholder rights are honored as much in the breach as in adherence. There is, moreover, a clear Russian preference for its own industry—most recently a resurgence of assertion by state-controlled firms. In short, despite the acquisition of [Russian oil company] TNK by British Petroleum, Russia may

1. According to the Energy Information Administration, output reached 8.8 million bpd in 2004.

find it difficult to attract the tens of billions of dollars in private investment necessary to make its ambitious oil expansion plans a reality.

And while the core of Russia's increased oil production has come from giant oil fields in Western Siberia, new investment is needed to exploit reserves in more remote areas including the Timon-Pechora region, eastern Siberia, the north Caspian Sea and the Russia Far East. Development of these distant resources is very important to Russia's future but faces technical, economic and bureaucratic barriers. Not only is the geographic terrain extremely challenging, but Russia's uncertain tax and legal regimes have created disincentives to foreign and even domestic investment in those ambitious new "greenfield" investments. Uncertainty about whether and under what incentives private companies will be able to invest in the future pipeline infrastructure needed to service these remote, but prolific oil fields has created apprehension as well. The United States has been pressing Russia to reform the state oil pipeline monopoly Transneft and its pipeline sector, but reform is slow in coming. . . .

Russian oil is relatively expensive, with much of the planned expansion in production slated for geographically remote and geologically challenging fields. This makes Russia's continued production expansion far more vulnerable to a sharp and sustained decline in oil prices than Persian Gulf production. Saudi Arabian oil, in contrast, is among the cheapest in the world to produce—allowing the Kingdom, at least potentially, to weather price declines with less pain. . . .

Iraq Is No Picnic, Either

With the removal of Saddam Hussein's regime, Iraq has joined Russia as a possible alternative to Saudi Arabia. Iraq possesses 11 percent of the world's proven oil reserves, second only to Saudi Arabia. While its oil sector never fully recovered from the disruption associated with the war with Iran and chronic

Sharpnack. © by Joe Sharpnack. Reproduced by permission.

under-investment during the 1980s, it nonetheless achieved production as high as 3.5 million bpd before the Gulf War of 1991. Under optimal circumstances, Iraq could be very attractive to foreign investors, not least because of its low production costs and proximity to both the Persian Gulf and Mediterranean Sea, giving it easy access to major European and Asian markets.

Some estimate that Iraqi oil production could reach 6–7 million bpd by the end of the decade, making it the world's third largest exporter after Saudi Arabia and Russia, and current plans are to reach 2.8 million bpd by 2005 and 5–6 million bpd sometime after 2010. But these estimates, while geologically possible, might prove to be optimistic for any number of political reasons. Whatever the ultimate course of the U.S. occupation of Iraq, it is clear that security will remain a concern for some time to come. Efforts to resume production since the war have already been hindered by widespread sabotage and lawlessness. Even returning production to the 2.5 million bpd level will represent a significant achievement given the vulnerability of oil production and transportation facilities in both the north and south of the country.

It will be expensive to expand Iraqi production, requiring either substantial foreign investment or high levels of foreign aid. At the best of times, Iraqi oil revenues only topped $10 to $12 billion dollars in recent years, with humanitarian assistance taking up 70 percent of those funds. Moreover, Iraq is far from offering the physical security, political stability and legal environment that will make it instantly attractive for major foreign investors. . . .

And will Iraq decide to opt out of OPEC? The idea that a grateful Iraqi citizenry will relinquish its rights to high oil prices out of gratitude to the United States for their liberation seems, to put it gently, farfetched. . . .

Other Sources, Other Problems

Even if, due to relatively poor global economic performance in recent years, the projection for world oil use by 2010 has been lowered from 100 billion bpd to 89 billion bpd, producing an additional 12 million bpd of oil—particularly in light of the constraints that Iraq and, to a lesser extent, Russia, face—will be no mean task. A quick *tour d'horizon* of oil producing regions reveals just how daunting that challenge will be. In Central Asia and the Caucasus, political instability, corruption, unstable customs, inadequate tax and legal regimes, as well as complex transportation issues (including problems created by Moscow), continue to be impediments to bringing major amounts of oil to market. Major increases in Latin

American oil output are similarly blocked by regulatory, political and environmental barriers. Faced with debilitating civil strife in Venezuela and a slowing pace of energy sector reform in important countries such as Brazil and Mexico, the United States will be forced to look elsewhere not just for increased oil imports, but even for the level of oil we have been receiving from our southern neighbors. Elsewhere, production in the North Sea is rapidly approaching its geological peak. And most of Asia remains very disappointing in terms of easily accessible, low-cost fields.

This means that, besides Russia (whose future is dependent on a stable investment and legal system not quite in place) the United States can expect to be most dependent on Africa for its increased need for oil imports. According to Baker Institute estimates, Africa, including North African producers such as Libya, could double output to 10 million bpd by 2010, alleviating some dependence on the Middle East. But, current political turmoil in West Africa, most notably in Nigeria and Angola, raises real questions about the reliability of already established African production.

Moreover, the United States faces a global competitor—China—that has an active place in Sudan's oil sector and has been pursuing a toehold elsewhere in the continent's oil wealth. Chinese participation in Africa has been accompanied in some cases by Chinese military delegations selling arms, a situation of some concern given the proclivity towards ethnic and political strife in some key oil producing countries in the region. East Asia frequently pulls one million bpd from West Africa to feed its growing appetite for high quality West African crude. . . .

What Are Our Options?

Our ability to shape production policies in Saudi Arabia, Russia and—in time—even Iraq is hugely constrained. In fact, the three countries may find ground for common production policy to sustain prices higher than optimal from America's perspective. Saudi Arabia remains, at least in theory, in a position to drive prices sufficiently low to compel Russian long-term production restraint. Given the importance of oil to Saudi Arabia's economy and finances, Riyadh would not undertake such a policy lightly. But it has done so before—not just against the Soviet Union in the 1980s, but more recently, against Venezuela in the late 1990s. . . .

Missing from this discussion are any serious measures to address the demand side of our reliance on Middle East oil. Current U.S. oil demand is about 20 million bpd, of which only 40 percent is produced domestically. Indeed, the consistent growth in U.S. oil imports is an overwhelming factor in global oil markets—one, which official Washington refuses to recognize despite criticism from allies in Europe and Japan. U.S. net imports rose from 6.79 million bpd in 1991 to 10.2 million bpd in 2000. Global oil trade, that is the amount of oil that is exported from one country to another, rose from 33.3 million bpd to 42.6 million bpd over that same period. This means that America's rising oil imports alone have represented over one third of the increase in oil traded worldwide over the past ten years—and over 50 percent of OPEC's output gains between the years 1991 to 2000 wound up in the United States. . . .

A shift to fuel cell technology and hydrogen-based technology, proposed by the Bush Administration and concretely pursued, may eventually reduce U.S. petroleum imports, but the time-frame involved runs to the decades, not years. Moreover, a hydrogen economy would be dependent upon scientific breakthroughs that are in no way guaranteed and would presume plentiful local natural gas supplies that are iffy, at best. Indeed, the administration's decision to focus on the "hydrogen economy" is viewed by many as an effort to deflect a more politically painful, but immediately plausible policy to make a here and now effort to switch to hybrid automotive technologies that could immediately reduce consumption through increased efficiency. General Motors' commitment to produce 1 million hydrogen fuel cell cars a year by 2012 seems pretty small when put up against the expectation of 100 million vehicle growth rate in the traditional gas-guzzling American transportation fleet over the same time period. . . .

A Necessary Supplier

Realistically, no matter what happens on the demand side in the United States, there is no escaping the need for increased overall world output to keeping prices reasonable despite rising world (and U.S.) demand. But the United States will do itself a disservice by indulging in the fantasy that it can create this supply by diplomatic pressure or military action. Like it or not, the maintenance of Saudi Arabia as a supplier of last resort is a necessary hedge against short- to medium-terms disruptions for which there is no replacement on the horizon. Over the course of the last year, such disruptions have occurred in both Venezuela and Nigeria. Far from replacing the U.S.-Saudi Arabian "special relationship" with an "axis of oil" between Moscow and Washington, the new approach can at best create an "oil triangle" with its points at Washington, Riyadh, and Moscow, perhaps eventually adding Baghdad or Ottawa into the mix.

| *"We don't have to be dependent on Arab regimes [for energy]."*

The United States Can Minimize Its Dependence on Middle East Oil

Robert McGarvey

While the United States cannot completely eliminate its depen-dence on foreign oil, it can reduce its dependence on oil from the Middle East, argues Robert McGarvey in the following view-point. McGarvey believes that diversification of energy sources is the key to reducing dependence. America should use nuclear power and burn coal, practice conservation, and import its oil from a variety of nations, he maintains. McGarvey is a freelance writer who lives in Arizona.

As you read, consider the following questions:

1. As explained by McGarvey, how does America's petro-leum reserve act as a deterrent to another Arab oil em-bargo?
2. According to the author, how much of its electricity does France get from nuclear power?
3. How many years of coal supplies lie underground in the United States, according to McGarvey?

Robert McGarvey, "U.S. Energy Independence: Salvation or Mirage?" *American Legion Magazine*, vol. 154, June 2003, pp. 24–26. Copyright © 2003 by Robert McGarvey. Re-produced by permission.

America is asking some serious energy questions. Can we count on Middle Eastern oil to power our cars, heat our homes and run our factories? Or should the United States go it alone, pursue a course of full-fledged energy independence, beholden to no foreign powers for oil?

These questions will linger long after the rebuilding of Iraq because the United States will continue to have enemies in the Middle East. Make no mistake: sentiments in favor of energy independence are showing up on the radar screens of policymakers. "You hear this especially inside the Beltway [the Washington, D.C., area]," says Jerry Taylor, an energy expert with the Cato Institute, a Washington-based think tank.

Energy Independence

What's not to like about energy self-sufficiency? At first-glance, it seems a brilliant goal, but understand that in many quarters "energy independence" are fighting words. Ask Lee Raymond, CEO of ExxonMobil, the world's largest petroleum company, about U.S. energy independence, and he snorts that the idea is "a delusion. It's just not realistic."

"Energy independence isn't a very attractive idea," agrees Luke Popovich, a spokesperson for the Alliance for Energy and Economic Growth, a Washington-based coalition of energy producers and users. "I don't think it is attainable."

Cato's Taylor is more blunt. If somehow the United States did achieve energy independence, he says, "it would be positively harmful. How would it be in the interest of U.S. national security to drain domestic reserves first?"

That's a troubling thought, but it's just one of many reasons why energy independence—as good an idea as it initially seems—has a number of critics.

Here's a reality check. Roughly 60 percent of the nation's petroleum now is imported. The first time Americans demanded energy independence was in the immediate aftermath of the 1973 Arab oil embargo, which cut off petroleum exports from October 1973 to March 1974. The result was chaos at the gas pumps, electricity brownouts, cold homes in the winter and an economy that stumbled, as national dependence upon abundant supplies of inexpensive energy became clear. The cure proposed by many in Washington was energy independence. So why is that call heard again 30 years later?

For good reason: the United States is more dependent than ever on foreign energy. At the time of the 1973 embargo, about 28 percent of the petroleum used in the United States came from foreign sources. U.S. dependence has since doubled. Why? Partly because imported oil "is cheaper than domestic," says Taylor, who explains that costs associated with production are low in, say, Saudi Arabia, but costs for drilling in the Alaskan interior would be much higher, both because of the remote location and the difficult environment. "Who would want to pay more for domestic oil simply because it is domestic?" Taylor asks.

At the same time, the nation's proven petroleum reserves have been dwindling. In 1972, the American Petroleum Institute—a Washington-based trade association—put domestic reserves at 36.3 billion barrels. In 2000, the U.S. Energy Information Administration pegged domestic reserves at 23.2 billion barrels. That number will likely keep falling because domestic fields are mature, and no one expects major new oil finds in the lower 48 states.

Does that spell doom for U.S. energy independence? Not exactly. "This country should do everything we reasonably can to attain our own energy security," says ExxonMobil's Raymond. "But let's not confuse that with the notion that we can be totally independent of the world."

"Already much is being done to ensure energy security," Popovich adds.

The fact is that in the 30 years since the first Arab oil embargo, the nation has taken dramatic steps to make itself impervious to foreign-energy threats:

Strong Petroleum Reserve

Government-owned fuel supplies have systematically built up during the George W. Bush administration. From 540 million barrels in 2000, the inventory expanded to 599 million barrels in January [2003], the highest level ever reached. How much fuel does this amount to? Best estimates are that this is ample petroleum to power the nation for about two months, and that, most experts believe, is a sizable deterrent to another Arab oil embargo. Keep in mind that Arab oil producers are highly dependent on the flow of U.S. dollars into their economies. They need that money as much as we need their energy, experts say.

Suppliers

The world now has many more places to shop for oil. Thirty years ago, OPEC [Organization of the Petroleum Exporting Countries]—a group primarily led by Middle-Eastern nations—dominated petroleum exports. Today, oil comes from a broad supplier base involving many non-OPEC countries such as Norway, the United Kingdom, Russia and Mexico. Experts are largely united in seeing non-OPEC nations stepping up production levels if a boycott were imposed by Arab nations. That means a 1973 embargo just couldn't happen again, experts say.

Higher Domestic Production

The United States may have dwindling domestic reserves, but sophisticated technologies are allowing oil companies to drill in places previously off-limits—particularly in the Gulf of Mexico. In a region 190 miles south of New Orleans, for instance, ChevronTexaco has tapped into a huge oil reserve in a region called the Tahitian Prospect. Drilling in water 4,000 feet deep—roughly four-fifths of a mile—ChevronTexaco probed another 28,411 feet before it hit pay-dirt. ExxonMobil,

Cutting Oil Consumption

It's entirely possible to cut projected U.S. oil consumption in half by 2025, and eliminate it completely by 2050, without compromising rapid economic growth. Demand could be halved simply by using oil twice as efficiently over several decades; the other half could be replaced with saved natural gas and advanced biofuels. . . .

Doubling oil efficiency wouldn't be hard. A backlog of powerful ways to save and substitute for oil, amassed since the 1973 oil embargo, remains mostly untapped, even in the most energy-efficient countries.

Amory B. Lovins, Newsweek, *August 8, 2005.*

too, is active in the gulf, as are many other companies. A decade ago, such wells were economically unthinkable and probably technologically impossible. Now they are almost commonplace and will contribute a rising flow of oil to meet the nation's needs.

Do these facts mean we already have energy independence? Nobody says that, but there is broad agreement that the United States may already have significant energy security because it is much less dependent on Arab oil than it was a generation ago.

The same experts also say more could be done to enhance domestic energy security if sufficient public support exists.

Nuclear Power

"It could generate all our electricity," says John Tobin, executive director of the Energy Literacy Project, an Evergreen, Colo., organization devoted to raising public awareness about energy issues. Nuclear power might be a 100-percent domestic resource, but it has been a political taboo for a quarter-century. Its supporters are scarce. But the rest of the world takes a more aggressive approach to nuclear power. France, for instance, gets 75 percent of its electricity from nuclear power, and Germany and Japan each get about 30 percent, compared to about 20 percent in the United States. "It's disappointing that we don't make more use of nuclear," Tobin says. However, nuclear power has a downside: worries about its safety. But, Tobin says, other nations believe they have a handle on this. Why can't the United States? The bottom line is more use of nuclear power remains a route to greater self-reliance only if the public and politicians unite in supporting it.

More Coal

"Burning more of it will help us be more energy independent," says Sam Tanenbaum, a professor of engineering at Harvey Mudd College in Claremont, Calif. The nation, which once burned coal as a primary source of energy, has enormous amounts of this fuel. Literally hundreds of years of supplies lie underground.

"There is more energy in coal reserves in Illinois alone than there is in all the oil of Saudi Arabia," says Steve Mc-Clure, CEO of Clearstack, a Springfield, Ill.–based company that researches technologies to allow for cleaner burning of coal. However, therein lies the rub. Coal is abundant but dirty. "I don't see any political will to significantly increase usage," Popovich says. Surprisingly enough, coal now amounts to more than 20 percent of the energy consumed in the United States. Mainly it is converted into electricity in Western states, but work such as Clearstack's is squarely aimed at making coal cleaner and therefore more usable.

Has progress been made? Studies underwritten by the Clean Coal Technology Program, a public-private joint venture run by the Department of Energy, already identify improvements in coal's cleanliness.

Conservation

Few believe we can conserve our way to energy independence. Abundant supplies of energy fuel a growing economy. But probably we soon will be able to "take steps to reduce our dependence on the internal-combustion engine (the automobile)," Tanenbaum says, and the less oil we need to run cars and trucks, the less we will need imported petroleum. How realistic are alternative-fuel vehicles?

Tanenbaum points to substantial improvements such as new-breed "hybrids," as they are called, from Toyota and Honda. These cars are primarily electricity-powered, and gasoline is used only as needed. Even more advanced research focuses on hydrogen-powered cars that will, in effect, produce their own power from the air around us. When will such cars be commonplace? Nobody is making hard predictions, but today's rate of innovation is faster, and more optimistic, than ever.

"We can take steps to raise our energy security, and we have been doing so," Popovich says. "Let's diversify our energy sources and in that way minimize our dependence on any one source. We don't have to be dependent on Arab regimes or any other regimes. Once we decide to, we can have the energy security we want. That is very possible."

"Governments . . . are increasingly taking control [of the oil industry]. And those governments often have interests quite hostile to ours."

China and Russia May Use Oil Interests to Threaten America's Global Power

Irwin M. Stelzer

In the following viewpoint Irwin M. Stelzer explains that China and Russia are both gaining influence in the worldwide oil market. Not only do these countries control vast deposits of oil, says Stelzer, but they are working with other oil-supplying nations to strengthen their power in the international community. He believes that China and Russia—and the alliances they forge— may threaten America's ability to obtain oil in the future. Stelzer is a contributing editor to the Weekly Standard, *director of economic policy studies at the Hudson Institute, and a columnist for the London* Sunday Times.

As you read, consider the following questions:

1. As cited by Stelzer, by how much did trade increase between Iran and China in 2000?

2. According to the author, how much has China agreed to

Irwin M. Stelzer, "The Axis of Oil," *Weekly Standard*, vol. 10, February 7, 2005, pp. 25–28. Copyright © 2005 by News Corporation, Weekly Standard. All rights reserved. Reproduced by permission.

invest in Venezuela's oil and gas industry?

3. How much of its oil and natural gas does Germany get from Russia, according to Stelzer?

A cold weather wave hits America's northeast, oil inventories are drawn down, and prices rise. A pipeline is blown up in Iraq, and prices rise even more. The OPEC [Organization of the Petroleum Exporting Countries] cartel meets and agrees to cut back production, adding to price pressures. The government announces a rise in inventories, or weather forecasters predict a thaw, or the Saudis say they will step up oil production, and prices fall. All interesting, all important to those playing the oil market or running companies that rely heavily on oil as an input, or trying to predict the course of their economies.

The U.S.-Saudi Relationship

But these hardy perennials of the business pages will soon seem trivial next to the structural changes occurring in the international oil industry. Start with the much-overlooked fact that President [George W.] Bush's inaugural address was nothing less than a repudiation of a deal cut 60 years ago by President Franklin Roosevelt [FDR] with Saudi king Ibn Saud. FDR took a detour en route to Washington from the Yalta conference to meet with Saud aboard the USS *Quincy*, anchored in the Great Bitter Lake in the Suez Canal. "The official record was surprisingly silent about what the two men said about oil," notes [author] Daniel Yergin in his magisterial *The Prize: The Epic Quest for Oil, Money & Power*, and Roosevelt died before he could make a full report. But no one doubted that the president had pledged U.S. support for the Saudi regime in return for Saud's promise of a steady flow of oil onto world markets.

It is certainly arguable that the Saudis reneged on their end of the bargain long before Bush decided to consign the

Bitter Lake arrangement to the dustbin of history. After all, their "guarantee" of a continued flow became inoperative when they joined the producers' embargo in 1973. More recently, they abandoned their reasonable-price pledge by allowing oil prices to shoot up without making any effort to expand production capacity. Nor can it be said that a regime that uses its oil revenues to fund the export of the virulent version of Islam that produced almost all of the terrorists who perpetrated the . . . September 11 [2001 terrorist attacks], and that pays bounties to the families of suicide bombers, is behaving in the way Roosevelt anticipated when he shook hands with Ibn Saud.

But if Saudi behavior is not a deal-breaker, George W. Bush's inaugural broadside against tyranny—against "governments with long habits of control"—certainly is, unless the long-standing Bush family relationship with the Saudis trumps the president's pledge. If Bush means what he says, and he usually does, he cannot favor the existing regime over such reform elements as might begin to emerge in Saudi Arabia. The kingdom will remain an important supplier of oil to the U.S. and world markets, and America will remain an important consumer of that oil, but it will be barrels-for-dollars from here on out, with no hidden promises to shore up the Saudi regime unless those threatening to replace it are an even greater threat to American interests. Which should please those eager to distance America from the odious House of Saud. . . .

A Changing Oil Market

The end, if that is what it is, of the U.S.-Saudi special relationship is only one of the profound changes that are occurring in the oil market. Other developments make a break with the Saudis even more risky than it would ordinarily be, as our supplies of oil become subject to a complicated set of international games. For we are witnessing what might be called the geopoliticization of the world's oil and gas industry.

Given past government interference, whether it was the Texas government trying to keep prices high by restricting output in the early days, or the OPEC cartel doing the same in recent times, it can't be said that the free play of supply and demand ever set prices in the oil market. But we are now seeing an even more profound uncoupling of the oil industry from anything resembling the model characteristic of market economies. Governments rather than traditional commercial enterprises are increasingly taking control. And those governments often have interests quite hostile to ours.

China

The Chinese are desperate to secure supplies of oil to sustain an economic growth rate that is crowding double digits and that converted them into a net importer of oil in 1993. That means, first of all, forging closer economic and political ties in the Middle East. The Iran-China Chamber of Commerce, established in 2000, reports that trade between the two countries totaled $7 billion last year [2004], a 25 percent increase over the previous year. But this is not the ordinary buying and selling of profit-driven companies. Instead, it is the result of state-owned companies in China buying oil from state-owned companies in Iran, in transactions aimed as much at mutual political advantage as at commerce. China buys oil and funds a U.S. adversary; Iran sells oil, and in return gets help with the nuclear weapons program that worries America. Score: Adversaries, 2; U.S., nil.

The China Petroleum & Chemical Company (Sinopec) also signed a 30-year natural gas purchase deal to help the mullahs get their gas industry moving and agreed to invest in the development of the Yadavaran oil field in return for Iran's agreement to sell it 150,000 barrels per day of crude oil. So much for U.S. trade sanctions.[1]

The advantages to Iran of closer ties with China are obviously not restricted to payments received for oil. As [journalists] Gal Luft and Anne Korin pointed out [in 2004] in *Commentary* [magazine], China "has sold ballistic-missile components to Iran as well as air-, land-, and sea-based cruise missiles. . . . Even more significantly, China has provided Iran with key ingredients for the development of nuclear weapons," and China's Fiber-Home Communications Technology is building a broadband network in Iran.

When Sinopec agreed to spend $300 million to develop natural gas resources in Saudi Arabia, "the deal raised eyebrows for its high risk and potentially low returns," reported the *New York Times*. Sure, the Chinese would like to find some natural gas. But most experts say that if Sinopec had to justify this transaction purely on commercial terms, as would an American company, the deal never would have been consummated. Or, as the *Wall Street Journal* puts it, "State-owned firms will have a higher risk appetite when buying assets than their listed counterparts." The Sinopec deal was aimed mainly at establishing a larger Chinese presence in the Middle East. And a market for products that are on America's list of embargoed items. The Sino-Saudi oil-for-arms trade has included the sale by China of ballistic missiles with a range of 1,800 miles and capable of carrying a nuclear warhead, according to Luft and Korin.

China clearly aims to position itself as an alternative to America as an ally and armorer of countries that oppose U.S. foreign policy. Amy Myers Jaffe, a fellow at the James A. Baker III Institute for Public Policy at Rice University, told the *New York Times* that the Chinese "tend toward countries where the U.S. has sanctions, like Sudan, Iran and Iraq." She might have

1. The U.S. government prohibits most trade with Iran.

added that China also tends towards countries that are key suppliers of the oil that keeps the wheels of American commerce turning.

China is not confining the extension of its influence to the Middle East. The Western Hemisphere is also in its sights. Canadian prime minister Paul Martin just visited Beijing and came away with a broad-ranging deal to cooperate in a wide variety of energy projects, including plans for a pipeline and ports that would allow as much as one million barrels per day of oil from Alberta's tar sands to move to Canada's west coast for export to China. That's one-third of the oil that America has been hoping might in the future be available to it from Canada's tar sands. . . .

Latin America

In Latin America, China has made a series of oil deals that extend its influence, and must have James Monroe[2] spinning in his grave. President Hu Jintao has agreed to invest $100 billion in Latin America in a variety of energy-related and other partnerships, as Latin American countries "try to lessen their trade dependence on the U.S.," according to reports in the *Wall Street Journal.*

Most threatening is the arrangement made with Venezuelan president Hugo Chávez, a man with close ties to [Cuban leader] Fidel Castro and who claims his country is under "a new U.S. imperialist attack." China has agreed to invest over $400 million in Venezuela's oil and gas industry, and to buy 120,000 barrels of that country's fuel oil each month. Chávez had made it known that he plans to use the proceeds of his oil industry to fund sales of cheap oil to Castro, and he has not denied rumors that he plans to finance revolutionary groups in other Latin American countries. Moreover, he has

2. The fifth U.S. president, Monroe was opposed to European colonization in Latin America.

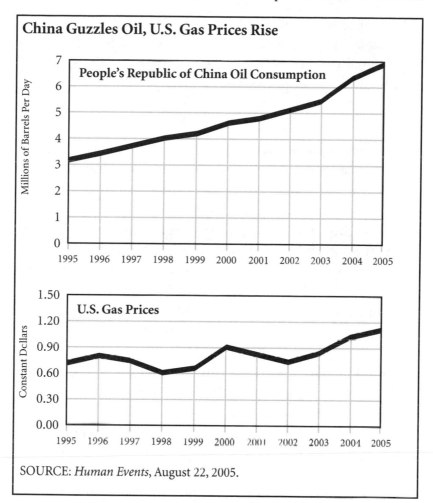

China Guzzles Oil, U.S. Gas Prices Rise

People's Republic of China Oil Consumption

U.S. Gas Prices

SOURCE: *Human Events*, August 22, 2005.

announced that he is no longer bound by his exploration and development deals with American companies ConocoPhillips, Harvest Natural Resources, and ChevronTexaco, putting into question the reliability of supplies from Venezuela, which account for 15 percent of U.S. imports.

To top off all of this, CNOOC, China's third largest oil company, is preparing a series of acquisitions in Asia that will allow China to acquire the resources it needs to fuel its growth and extend its influence into countries in which its commercial presence has until now been insignificant. Most notable is a probable $13 billion takeover of Unocal, to be followed by the disposal of Unocal's American assets but the retention of its substantial Asian properties.

Russia

Meanwhile, [Russian president] Vladimir Putin has been developing what astute observer [journalist] Roger Boyes calls "a new policy instrument" to reassert Russian power. That instrument is "the Russian gas and oil-exporting companies that already all but dominate Europe's energy supplies. . . . [Russian natural gas company] Gazprom has woven a web of energy dependencies from Turkey to Turkmenistan, from Berlin to Baku." According to the International Energy Agency, by 2020, natural gas will account for 62 percent of Europe's energy consumption, and Russia will supply two-thirds of that gas.

This domination has more than commercial consequences. When German chancellor Gerhard Schröder told a television audience that Putin is a "dyed-in-the-wool democrat," the uninitiated chuckled, but insiders knew that the chancellor was simply indicating that he is not prepared to bite the hand that controls the valves of the pipelines that warm his country. Germany already gets 35 percent of its oil and 40 percent of its gas from Russia, figures that will steadily increase as Germany pursues its policy of winding down its nuclear power industry. The head of one of the think tanks affiliated with the German government preferred to remain anonymous when he told the press, "Given Moscow's history of strong-arming neighbors, we might want to think whether we really want to be in such a relationship."

Russia also plans to use its ample reserves of oil and gas to extend its influence in Asia. It has already agreed to allow Japan to finance an oil pipeline from eastern Siberia to the Pacific, from where it can be transported to Japan. The line, to be built by Russia's Transneft, will cover some 2,600 miles, cost $11.5 billion (some put the price tag at closer to $18 billion), and allow Russia to export to several Asian nations as well as Japan. This was no mere commercial transaction: Japanese prime minister Junichiro Koizumi led the lobbying team that persuaded Putin to select the route that Japan favored.

Perhaps most important is Russia's use of oil to cement relations with China, an emerging alliance the consequences of which [political columnist] Charles Krauthammer has already warned are dangerous to American interests. A few weeks ago [in early 2005] Russian energy minister Viktor Krishtenko visited Beijing to discuss areas of mutual interest with his Chinese counterparts. Just how China's desire to secure supplies of oil and natural gas, and Russia's desire for new markets and strategic advantage, will play out is uncertain. But there is every sign that Russian fuel is starting to warm historically chilly Sino-Russian relations. Putin has offered the China National Petroleum Corporation a piece of Yukos, the Russian oil giant that produces 1 percent of the world's crude oil, and that Putin effectively renationalized by jailing its principal shareholder (a Putin political opponent), and then slapping the company with a bankrupting demand for back taxes. Since American companies would have loved to have a crack at an interest in Yukos, Putin's decision to freeze them out is widely seen as a political decision to express unhappiness with American criticism of his recent power grabs, as well as an opportunity to cement relations with China, with which Russia's Gazprom already has signed agreements to cooperate in oil and gas markets.

Once again, we are witnessing deals that are more political than economic. Putin's *siloviki* [politicians], which includes his old KGB [the former Soviet intelligence agency] chums, is now firmly in control of Russia's oil industry, and plans to use the nation's resources to further diplomatic as well as economic goals, with the former taking precedence over the latter if the two goals should clash. As the *Economist* put it in a story titled "KGB Inc.," "It is a quirk of Russian history that the country's best hope of recovering the influence lost by Moscow with the fall of the Soviet Union is through the energy business." Former spies and "Kremlin henchmen," the story continued, quoting Paul Collison, an energy analyst at Brunswick UBS (a Russia-focused investment house), will make decisions in the interests of "only one shareholder—the state." . . .

Something to Worry About

So picture this web of influence that is being woven by countries eager to constrain American power. Canada and China become joint venturers, as do Venezuela and China. Canada is America's largest source of imported oil, and Venezuela sells us the light, sweet crude oil that our refineries are best equipped to handle. This means that a significant portion of the incremental production from these countries—and perhaps some of what is now headed here—goes to China, rather than to the United States, as energy planners here have been assuming. More important, no one believes that these deals are strictly economic, or would meet shareholder approval were such a force present in China. These are deals by state agencies, designed to extend China's influence to corners of the world from which it has until now been absent.

China has also solidified relations with Iran and other countries on America's list of international pariahs, trading arms for oil, and using its financial clout to establish close diplomatic ties in the region that contains the largest reserves of oil and gas in the world.

Meanwhile, Russia is using its reserves to dominate the European energy market, and make Germany, France, and other countries heavily dependent on Putin's good will. Not that he would cut off supplies at the slightest provocation. He doesn't have to. All the Russian "dyed-in-the-wool democrat" has to do is rely on German and French self-interest to tip those countries to his side in any dispute with the United States, just as China can rely on Latin American countries that benefit from its billions of investment to give that fact some weight in formulating their foreign policies.

Add the emerging relationship of China and Russia, and you have something to worry about.

"A crucial part of combating the spread of Wahhabism is combating [the] growing thirst for oil."

Saudi Arabia Is Using Oil to Spread Islamic Fundamentalism

Joseph Braude

Saudi Arabia uses the profits made from selling oil to finance terrorists, according to Joseph Braude in the following viewpoint. As more Middle Eastern nations become dependent on Saudi Arabian oil, he claims, Saudi Arabia is gaining power in the region, which is resulting in the spread of militant Islamist beliefs. In Braude's opinion, in order to combat the spread of this ideology, the United States should help Middle Eastern countries become independent of Saudi Arabia by developing alternative sources of energy. Braude is the author of The New Iraq: Rebuilding the Country for Its People, the Middle East, and the World.

As you read, consider the following questions:

1. In the author's opinion, why has Tunisia resisted foreign meddling in its local Islamic culture?

2. How is the automotive industry changing in the Middle East, in Braude's opinion?

Joseph Braude, "Oil-for-Feud—the Greening of the Middle East," *The New Republic*, July 4, 2004. Copyright © 2005 by The New Republic, Inc. Reproduced by permission.

3. According to the author, why are alternative energy sources such as solar power more likely to be successful in the Middle East than in the United States?

You've heard it plenty of times: The Saudis are exporting Islamist militancy throughout the Middle East and beyond, and Americans are picking up the tab, with the $30 billion we spend annually on Saudi oil helping to finance fundamentalist mosques and madrassas [Islamic schools]. "We are financing both sides in the war on terrorism," observed [columnist] Thomas L. Friedman in a March [2005] *New York Times* column. And we're doing so faster than ever, because oil now fetches nearly $60 a barrel—more than twice the pre–September 11 [2001] price. The only solution, experts say, is to spend less on fossil fuel and more on renewable energy—a double whammy of environmentalism and power politics that Friedman has dubbed the "geo-green strategy." Cutting dependence on foreign oil is "America's best weapon against terrorism," argues the Institute for the Analysis of Global Security (a hawkish think tank whose energy proposals have been backed by green groups like the Natural Resources Defense Council). The group says it would "invalidate the social contract between the leaders and their people and stem the flow of resources to the religious establishment."

Americans would do well to follow this advice. Burning less oil would protect the environment and could strengthen the economy, while the quest for viable alternatives would inspire a new generation of scientists and entrepreneurs. But, as a tactic for ending Saudi-sponsored militancy, the geo-green strategy won't work for the foreseeable future. Even if Americans dramatically reduced their spending on foreign oil, the ensuing void in Saudi coffers would readily be filled by new oil-starved customers to the east, notably China and India. Saudi Arabia and its clerical elite will remain rich, no matter how many Americans drive a Prius [hybrid vehicle].

Using Oil for Political Influence

But that's only part of the problem. Worse is the fact that a growing number of Middle Eastern countries are themselves in line to become net oil importers—and they, too, will be buying from Saudi Arabia. This trend is bad news for Americans and good news for extremist Saudi clerics, because, in the Middle East, wherever oil flows, ideas tend to follow. Fortunately, there are remedies to the problem, such as deploying existing renewable-energy technologies to oil-poor Arab countries. Unfortunately, rather than adopt such an approach, the United States is standing on the sidelines while these countries boost their demand for oil—and bolster Saudi soft power and extremist Islamism in the process.

Petrodollars buy more political influence in the Middle East today than ever before, because there are fewer regimes that dole them out. [Former Iraqi president Saddam Hussein's] Iraq used to fund journalists, politicians, and terrorists in various Arab countries—it delivered pro-Iraqi rallies in Egypt and Jordan, assassinations in Lebanon and Syria, life insurance policies for suicide bombers in Palestine, and even an unsuccessful coup attempt in Mauritania in the late '90s. But those days are, of course, now over. In the 1980s and early '90s, Iran paid Islamists to destabilize the secular Arab governments in Tunisia, Algeria, and Egypt. But, after the Iran-Iraq war, the Iranian mullahs agreed to cease and desist in exchange for normalized relations with Arab rulers. Iran still supports Shia Islamists in Lebanon and Iraq and terrorism against Israel, but, for the most part, it has stopped meddling in Sunni Arab affairs. Oil-rich Libya, though always a wild card, is largely restrained from funding foreign mischief by its ruler's desire for detente with the Bush administration. All these changes leave aspiring Sunni firebrands with one place to grub for cash: Saudi Arabia.

The Saudis have exported ideology throughout the Middle East for decades. In the 1960s and 1970s, the Saudi monarchy was on the defensive against Egyptian President Gamal Abdel Nasser's pan-Arab nationalism, which tried to persuade Arab societies to overthrow their dynasties and kings. In response, Saudi Arabia gave clerics money to spread a strident brand of Sunni puritanism that delegitimized Nasser's secular ideology—and secularism in general. This 20-year battle of ideas essentially ended in a draw: Arabism became the cult of most Arab regimes, but Saudi-backed Wahhabism became the ideology of many, if not most, Sunni mosques. In the '80s and '90s, the Saudi regime used the soft-power network it had built to go on the offensive, taking aim at the region's godless dissidents. These efforts largely worked: Socialists in Egypt lost ground to the Saudi-backed Muslim Brotherhood, and the Palestinian Liberation Organization lost ground to the Saudi-backed Hamas.

But, on September 11—roughly 40 years after Saudi money began to flood foreign mosques—bin Ladenism put the oil-rich kingdom back on the defensive. Ironically, bin Ladenism is a product of the brand of Islamic extremism preached in Saudi mosques in the '70s and '80s. Like Nasser, [terrorist] Osama bin Laden has taken aim at the legitimacy of Arab monarchs (beginning with those who rule his native Saudi Arabia), railing against their corruption and pro-Western tilt. By doing so, he has forced the kingdom back into the mosque-wooing business, at home as well as abroad. The Saudi government-backed Muslim World League and other clerical endowments continue to finance mosques and seminaries in every Arab country. While these mosques eschew outright incitement against Arab regimes, the message they propagate is bin Laden–like in the virulence of its denunciation of Western influence and ideals. The effect is to incubate intolerance and violence against Christians, Jews, and Americans.

Jordan and Tunisia

Consider the case of Jordan, the country that spawned Iraq's Al Qaeda [terrorist group] chief, Abu Musab Al Zarqawi. There's nothing appealing to Jordan's King Abdullah about the enormous influence Saudi radicals wield over many of his country's mosques. But Abdullah depends on Saudi Arabia for cheap, subsidized oil; he has none of his own. So there are limits to what he can do to stem the flow of Saudi soft power into his country. Hardly a friend of freedom and democracy, Jordan's king is increasingly viewed in Washington as a disappointment on the issue of political reform. If you're a secular liberal and want to start a national party in Amman, you're in for a rough fight. But, when Saudi-backed preachers play politics in the country's mosques—even, at times, campaigning against the king's own pro-Western policies—Abdullah suddenly shows off his tolerance for pluralism. At an April [2005] conference of the pro-Saudi Salafi movement in Amman, local and foreign preachers, including a guest from Saudi Arabia, spoke out against Jews, Christians, Shia, feminism, and globalization. Sheik Muhammad Nasr denounced the latter as a "scourge" and an "American-led plot to disrupt Muslim unity." These sentiments aren't exactly simpatico to an authoritarian state with a ubiquitous queen, a warm peace with Israel, a large urban Christian community, a Shia refugee population, and membership in the World Trade Organization. Yet the clerics who delivered these tirades were left alone by the government. When Jordanian Christian dissident Ali Hattar expressed similar anti-Western sentiments in December [2004], however, he was persecuted by the secret police. The difference? Salafi clerics are staunchly backed by Saudi Arabia, and Saudi Arabia is indispensable to the Jordanian economy.

Contrast Jordan with Tunisia, another authoritarian Arab state with a poor human rights record. Dissidents are no better off in Tunis than they are in Amman. But there's a key dif-

Another September 11?

Saudi Arabia is still the largest sponsor and supporter of Islamic terrorism in the world. Spreading the Wahhabi Cult across the Muslim world (including many Muslims in America) and teaching hate and intolerance, even of non-Wahhabi Muslims. The hate being taught in schools and mosques must be ended. The American "crack whore" addiction to cheap oil must end or we will continue to sell-out everything we stand for just to get the next fix. $3 a gallon for gas is cheaper than the next September 11.

Lewis Loflin, 2005. www.sullivan-country.com.

ference as far as the war on terrorism is concerned: In Tunis—which maintains a modest oil supply of its own and, until recently, was a net oil exporter—Saudi-style firebrands aren't tolerated. The leadership keeps close tabs on the messages emanating from its mosques and shows little patience with foreign meddling in the local Islamic culture. In 1995, the government went so far as to reengineer the curriculum of the historic Zaitouna Islamic seminary, introducing a new focus on coming to grips with modernity and teaching tolerance of Jews, Christians, and diverse schools of Islamic thought—a stark difference from the intolerance preached in Saudi-backed madrassas. The Tunisian state has been committed to fostering religious pluralism and secularism for decades—decades during which the country enjoyed energy independence, and hence political independence, from oil exporters to the east.

Unfortunately, many Arab countries are running low on oil, or running out of it entirely, while their populations grow and consumption habits swell. In short, the region is becoming more like Jordan and less like Tunisia—a boon for future Zarqawis, a blow to tolerance. There are no known oil reserves in

Palestine or Lebanon. Syria, according to the U.S. government's Energy Information Administration, is due to exhaust its oil supply within the next ten years. Egypt's production has been steadily declining while its population has been skyrocketing; domestic demand for oil will outstrip production by—according to more bearish predictions—as early as 2010. In Yemen, a modest oil producer, domestic demand has been growing at the staggering rate of 9 percent annually. What all this means is that America's primary Arab targets for democratization are also increasingly vulnerable to Saudi-backed Wahhabi Islamization. And say what you will about Islam's potential to coexist with democracy, there's no denying that Saudi-style Islamism abhors democracy. As Wahhabi preacher Muhammad Nasr said at the April powwow in Amman: "Islam is a nation of unity. Diversity is the slogan of the infidels. . . . And party politics are the root cause of the weakness of the [Islamic] nation."

Future Growth Predictions

If you're an optimist, you can point out that oil dependency forecasts should always be taken with a grain of salt. A new refinery or two can significantly alter the calculations, and some of the increased demand from consumers at the pumps can be offset by replacing oil with natural gas to power a country's electric plants. Egypt, for example, is making such a transition now. These arguments would be reasonable in the West, but, in the Middle East, they are neutralized by several added factors.

First, the Middle East's demographic growth is incomparable to almost any other region of the world—its population is expected to double in 25 years. Second, not only is the number of automobile drivers growing; the size and gasoline consumption of the vehicles they drive are growing, too. Iran's automotive industry, which used to export matchbox-size cars to Syria and Yemen, now produces mainly midsize sedans and minivans, in addition to new fleets of minibuses and trucks. Nissan announced in April that its Cairo factory has begun to manufacture pickup trucks for local distribution and regional export, and, for the first time, the company will export SUVs [sport utility vehicles] to Egypt. Third, Arab governments—often under U.S. corporate tutelage—tend to favor roads over rail lines when drawing up transportation blueprints. Witness Morocco, whose highway traffic increased 18 percent between 2003 and 2004 and whose highway network is to be expanded from its current 550 kilometers to 1,500 kilometers by 2010. Apparently, the one American-style freedom Arab governments have concrete plans to establish is the freedom of the open road.

Renewable Energy Projects

A crucial part of combating the spread of Wahhabism is combating this growing thirst for oil. One might assume that efforts to reduce oil consumption wouldn't work in the Middle East; after all, in the United States, most environmentally friendly power plants are hydroelectric, and, obviously, water in the Middle East is scarce. But third rate power sources in the United States happen to have first-rate potential in Arab countries: Where there's fierce desert wind, 300 days of sunlight per year, and natural hot springs, solar, wind, and geothermal energy are a big deal. Just ask the new Center for Solar Energy in Yemen, which is agitating for money and resources to set up sun-powered facilities all over that country. "Almighty God," the Center reports, "has bestowed upon Yemen an abundant share of the quantity of solar energy. The solar energy that descends upon the [average] single square meter of Yemen is considered to be among the highest averages in the world." Or talk to the team of scientists from Beirut, Amman, and Damascus who came together [in 2004] to carry out an exhaustive assessment of wind, solar, and biomass technology applications in their three countries. The study found that their electricity demand had roughly doubled over the past ten years—a trend that is forecast to continue over the next ten years—and faulted the region's electricity production for being unnecessarily dependent on oil-fueled plants. "Renewable energy use in the three countries," the study argues, "will result in important savings of fossil fuels. . . . Such savings would help limit the growth of energy imports and hence save on energy expenditures."

A common theme in the region's renewable energy projects is that they bring together countries that don't otherwise get along in pursuit of a constructive common agenda, giving them additional value. Last month [June 2005], for example, Israel, the Palestinian Authority, and Jordan agreed to jointly study the possibility of building a canal linking the Red Sea to the Dead Sea that could power a desalination plant; the study will be funded by the World Bank. Alas, another thing these initiatives tend to have in common is the absence of the United States. Last year's Middle East & North Africa Renewable Energy Conference, held in Sanaa, Yemen, was jointly sponsored by the Yemeni government and the German Ministry of the Environment. Italy recently signed an agreement with Tunisia and Morocco to boost work on renewable energy as part of the Euromediterranean Space for Education and Research. A Greek initiative on alternative fuel sources for the Mediterranean basin brings together seven Arab states with France, Italy, Portugal, and Spain. These projects serve the ultimate goal of weaning Arab countries off fossil fuel, but they also pay dividends for their European members, by scoring goodwill and public diplomacy points in Arab countries. The U.S. government has the technical resources and expertise to join and even lead these ventures—yet, far too often, it is not involved at all.

One American who understands the strategic value of sharing U.S. energy innovation with Arab countries is Robert Freling, director of the Washington-based Solar Electric Light

Fund. The group brings solar power, telephony, and Internet access to rural villages in the developing world. According to Freling, one of his ventures—a project in northern Nigeria that received funding from the U.S. Agency for International Development (USAID)—was widely covered in the African press and led to further requests from Morocco, Egypt, Jordan, Syria, and Yemen, among other countries. But Freling says he has not been able to grant any of these requests, because USAID has declined to fund them.

Encouraging Energy Independence

The U.S. government should adopt a far-reaching plan to deploy these and other technologies to energy-poor Arab countries as part of a broader effort to stem the Middle East's growing dependency on Saudi largesse. Energy independence, though a distant vision for the United States, is a viable goal for much of the Arab world. In recognition of the link between freedom from oil and prospects for political reform, the State Department's Middle East Partnership Initiative should promote renewable energy. The Commerce Department should aggressively court renewable energy start-up companies—and adopt a policy of fostering their promotion in the Middle East. USAID should fund joint ventures between American and Arab scientists and entrepreneurs for wind and solar technology applications in sun-drenched desert environments. The Bush administration should help Arab governments phase out oil-fueled power plants in favor of natural gas and other alternatives. The White House should also push U.S. construction companies that do business in the Middle East, such as Halliburton, to urge Arab governments to build rails instead of roads. Needless to say, in all these endeavors, the United States should also lead by example.

To be sure, the flow of oil is not the only factor that affects the symbiotic relationship between Saudi Arabia and its less well-off Arab neighbors. But the energy dependence of

Jordan and many of its neighbors has an appreciable political impact. Which is why the geo-green strategy to fight Islamic fundamentalism is a noble idea that won't work unless it is applied in Arab countries as well as at home. It is vital to U.S. interests that oil not be the Arab world's fuel of choice, lest Wahhabism become its ideology of choice.

> *"Most Central Asians believe that US antiterror troops are stationed in their region mainly to secure American oil interests."*

America Is Using the War on Terror to Further Its Oil Interests in Central Asia

Lutz Kleveman

In the following viewpoint Lutz Kleveman argues that the United States has dramatically increased its military presence in Central Asia in order to gain control of oil reserves there. He believes that America has taken this action under the guise of fighting terrorism. Ironically, says Kleveman, the U.S. presence in that region is actually fueling terrorism. By propping up unpopular and brutal regimes, the United States is spreading unrest and anti-Americanism, says Kleveman, both of which fuel terrorists. He advises that a better policy would be for the United States to begin reducing its dependence on oil. Kleveman is the author of The New Great Game: Blood and Oil in Central Asia.

As you read, consider the following questions:

1. By 2010, what is the potential oil production of the Caspian region, according to the author?

2. According to Kleveman, how has Russia reacted to America's military presence in Central Asia?

3. In the author's opinion, what has been the effect of oil on the common people in all oil-producing countries?

About a year ago [in 2003] I visited the US air base in Bagram, some thirty miles north of the Afghan capital of Kabul. A US Army public affairs [PA] officer, a friendly Texan, gave me a tour of the sprawling camp, set up after the ouster of the Taliban[1] in December 2001. It was a clear day, and one Chinook helicopter after the other took off to transport combat troops into the nearby mountains. As we walked past the endless rows of tents and men in desert camouflage uniforms, I spotted a wooden pole carrying two makeshift street signs. They read "Exxon Street" and "Petro Boulevard." Slightly embarrassed, the PA officer explained, "This is the fuel handlers' workplace. The signs are obviously a joke, a sort of irony."

As I am sure it was. It just seemed an uncanny sight, as I was researching the potential links between the "war on terror" and American oil interests in Central Asia. I had already traveled thousands of miles from the Caucasus peaks across the Caspian Sea and the Central Asian plains all the way down to the Afghan Hindu Kush. On that journey I met with and interviewed warlords, diplomats, politicians, generals and oil bosses. They are all players in a geostrategic struggle that has become increasingly intertwined with the war on terror: the new "Great Game."

The Great Game

In this rerun of the first "Great Game," the nineteenth-century imperial rivalry between the British Empire and czarist Russia, powerful players once again position themselves to control the heart of the Eurasian landmass, left in a post-Soviet power

---

1. An Islamist group that ruled most of Afghanistan from 1996 until it was removed by a U.S.-led coalition in 2001.

vacuum. Today the United States has taken over the leading role from the British. Along with the ever-present Russians, new regional powers such as China, Iran, Turkey and Pakistan have entered the arena, and transnational oil corporations are also pursuing their own interests in a brash, Wild East style.

Since September 11, 2001, the Bush Administration has undertaken a massive military buildup in Central Asia, deploying thousands of US troops not only in Afghanistan but also in the newly independent republics of Uzbekistan, Kyrgyzstan and Georgia. These first US combat troops on former Soviet territory have dramatically altered the geostrategic power equations in the region, with Washington trying to seal the cold war victory against Russia, contain Chinese influence and tighten the noose around Iran. Most important, however, the Bush Administration is using the "war on terror" to further American energy interests in Central Asia. The bad news is that this dramatic geopolitical gamble involving thuggish dictators and corrupt Saudi oil sheiks is likely to produce only more terrorists, jeopardizing America's prospects of defeating the forces responsible for the September 11 [terrorist] attacks.

Caspian Energy Reserves

The main spoils in today's Great Game are the Caspian energy reserves, principally oil and gas. On its shores, and at the bottom of the Caspian Sea, lie the world's biggest untapped fossil fuel resources. Estimates range from 85 to 219 billion barrels of crude, worth up to $4 trillion. According to the US Energy Department, Azerbaijan and Kazakhstan alone could sit on more than 110 billion barrels, more than three times the US reserves. Oil giants such as ExxonMobil, ChevronTexaco and British Petroleum [BP] have already invested more than $30 billion in new production facilities.

The aggressive US pursuit of oil interests in the Caspian did not start with the Bush Administration but during the Clinton years, with the Democratic President personally conducting oil and pipeline diplomacy with Caspian leaders. Despite Clinton's failure to reduce the Russian influence in the region decisively, American industry leaders were impressed. "I cannot think of a time when we have had a region emerge as suddenly to become as strategically significant as the Caspian," declared Dick Cheney in 1998 in a speech to oil industrialists in Washington. Cheney was then still CEO [chief executive officer] of the oil-services giant Halliburton. In May 2001 Cheney, now US Vice President, recommended in the Administration's seminal National Energy Policy report that "the President make energy security a priority of our trade and foreign policy," singling out the Caspian Basin as a "rapidly growing new area of supply." Keen to outdo Clinton's oil record, the Bush Administration took the new Great Game into its second round.

With potential oil production of up to 4.7 million barrels per day by 2010, the Caspian region has become crucial to the US policy of "diversifying energy supply." The other major supplier is the oil-rich Gulf of Guinea, where both the Clinton and the Bush administrations have vigorously developed US oil interests and strengthened ties with corrupt West African regimes. The strategy of supply diversification, originally designed after the 1973 oil shock,[2] is designed to wean America off its dependence on the Arab-dominated OPEC [Organization of the Petroleum Exporting Countries] cartel, which has been using its near-monopoly position as pawn and leverage against industrialized countries. As global oil consumption keeps surging and many oil wells outside the Middle East are nearing depletion, OPEC is in the long run going to expand its share of the world market even further. At the same time, the United States will have to import more than two-thirds of its total energy needs by 2020, mostly from the volatile Middle East.

2. when Arab members of OPEC stopped oil supplies to the United States, causing an economic crisis.

Looking for Alternatives

Many people in Washington are particularly uncomfortable with the growing power of Saudi Arabia, whose terror ties have been exposed since the September 11 terror attacks. As the recent bombings in Riyadh[3] have shown, there is a growing risk that radical Islamist groups will topple the corrupt Saud dynasty, only to then stop the flow of oil to "infidels." The consequences of 8 million barrels of oil—10 percent of global production—disappearing from the world markets overnight would be disastrous. Even without any such anti-Western revolution, the Saudi petrol is already, as it were, ideologically contaminated. To stave off political turmoil, the regime in Riyadh funds the radical Islamic Wahhabi sect, many of whose preachers call for terror against Americans around the world.

To get out of its Faustian pact with Saudi Arabia, the United States has tried to reduce its dependence on Saudi oil sheiks by seeking to secure access to other sources. Central Asia, however, is no less volatile than the Middle East, and oil politics are only making matters worse: Fierce conflicts have broken out over pipeline routes from the landlocked Caspian region to high-sea ports. Russia, still regarding itself as the imperial overlord of its former colonies, promotes pipeline routes across its territory, notably Chechnya, in the North Caucasus. China, the increasingly oil-dependent waking giant in the region, wants to build eastbound pipelines from Kazakhstan. Iran is offering its pipeline network for exports via the Persian Gulf.

By contrast, both the Clinton and Bush administrations have championed two pipelines that would circumvent both Russia and Iran. One of them, first planned by the US oil company Unocal in the mid-1990s, would run from Turk-

3. In May 2003, three compounds in the Saudi capital city of Riyadh that contained large numbers of Americans and Westerners were bombed. The terrorist group Al Qaeda is believed responsible.

menistan through Afghanistan to the Pakistani port of Gwadar on the Indian Ocean. Several months after the US-led overthrow of the Taliban regime, Afghan President Hamid Karzai, a former Unocal adviser, signed a treaty with Pakistani leader Pervez Musharraf and the Turkmen dictator Saparmurat Niyazov to authorize construction of a $3.2 billion gas pipeline through the Herat-Kandahar corridor in Afghanistan, with a projected capacity of about 1 trillion cubic feet of gas per year. A feasibility study is under way, and a parallel pipeline for oil is also planned for a later stage. So far, however, continuing warlordism in Afghanistan has prevented any private investor from coming forward.

Construction has already begun on a gigantic $3.6 billion oil pipeline from Azerbaijan's capital of Baku via neighboring Georgia to Turkey's Mediterranean port of Ceyhan. British Petroleum Amoco, its main operator, has invested billions in oil-rich Azerbaijan and can count on firm political support from the Bush Administration, which stationed about 500 elite troops in war-torn Georgia in May 2002. Controversial for environmental and social reasons, as it is unlikely to alleviate poverty in the notoriously corrupt transit countries, the pipeline project also perpetuates instability in the South Caucasus. With thousands of Russian troops still stationed in Georgia and Armenia, Moscow has for years sought to deter Western pipeline investors by fomenting bloody ethnic conflicts near the pipeline route, in the Armenian enclave of Nagorno-Karabakh in Azerbaijan and in the Georgian breakaway regions of Abkhazia, South Ossetia and Ajaria.

Russia's Reaction

Washington's Great Game opponents in Moscow and Beijing resent the dramatically growing US influence in their strategic backyard. Worried that the American presence might encourage internal unrest in its Central Asian province of Xinjiang—whose Turkic and Muslim population, the Uighurs, are striving for more autonomy—China has recently held joint military exercises with Kyrgyzstan.

The Russian government initially tolerated the American intrusion into its former empire, hoping Washington would in turn ignore Russian atrocities in Chechnya.[4] However, for the Kremlin, the much-hyped "new strategic partnership" against terror between the Kremlin and the White House has always been little more than a tactical and temporary marriage of convenience to allow Russia's battered economy to recover with the help of capital from Western companies. The US presence in Russia's backyard is becoming ever more assertive, but it is unthinkable for the majority of the Russian establishment to permanently cede its hegemonic claims on Central Asia.

One man who is quite frank about this is Viktor Kalyuzhny, the Russian deputy foreign minister and President Vladimir Putin's special envoy to the Caspian region, whom I interviewed in Moscow [in 2003]. "We have a saying in Russia," he told me. "If you have guests in the house there are two times when you are happy. One is when they arrive, and one is when they leave again." To make sure that I got the message, Kalyuzhny added, "Guests should know that it is impolite to stay for too long."

Unfazed by such Russian sensitivities, American troops in Central Asia seem to be there to stay. [In 2002], when I visited the new US air base in Kyrgyzstan, I was struck by the massive commitment the Pentagon had made. With the help of dozens of excavators, bulldozers and cranes, a pioneer unit was busy erecting a new hangar for F/A-18 Hornet fighter jets. Brawny pioneers in desert camouflage were setting up hundreds of "Harvest Falcon" and "Force Provider" tents for nearly 3,000 soldiers. I asked their commander, a wiry brigadier gen-

4. During the collapse of the Soviet Union, the republic of Chechnya declared independence. This independence has not been recognized and there have been numerous armed conflicts between Chechen groups and the Russian army, resulting in thousands of deaths.

eral, if and when the troops would ever leave Kyrgyzstan. "There is no time limit," he replied. "We will pull out only when all Al Qaeda [terrorist] cells have been eradicated."

Today, the troops are still there and many tents have been replaced by concrete buildings. Increasingly annoyed, Russian Defense Minister Sergei Ivanov has repeatedly demanded that the Americans pull out within two years. Significantly, President Putin has signed new security pacts with the Central Asian rulers and [in] October [2003] personally opened a new Russian military base in Kyrgyzstan. It is the first base Moscow has set up outside Russia's borders since the end of the cold war. Equipped with fighter jets, it lies only twenty miles away from the US air base.

Fueling Terrorism

Besides raising the specter of interstate conflict, the Bush Administration's energy imperialism jeopardizes the few successes in the war on terror. That is because the resentment US policies cause in Central Asia makes it easier for Al Qaeda–like organizations to recruit new fighters. They hate America because in its search for antiterrorist allies in the new Great Game, the Bush Administration has wooed some of the region's most brutal autocrats, including Azerbaijan's Heydar Aliyev, Kazakhstan's Nursultan Nazarbayev and Pakistan's Musharraf.

The most tyrannical of Washington's new allies is Islom Karimov, the ex-Communist dictator of Uzbekistan, who allowed US troops to set up a large and permanent military base on Uzbek soil during the Afghan campaign in late 2001. Ever since, the Bush Administration has turned a blind eye to the Karimov regime's brutal suppression of opposition and Islamic groups. "Such people must be shot in the head. If necessary, I will shoot them myself," Karimov once famously told his rubber-stamp Parliament.

Military Oil Protection

The use of American military personnel to help protect vulnerable oil installations in conflict-prone, chronically unstable countries is certain to expand given three critical factors: America's ever-increasing dependence on imported petroleum, a global shift in oil production from the developed to the developing world, and the growing militarization of our foreign energy policy.

Michael T. Klare, Human Quest, *November/December 2004.*

Although the US State Department acknowledges that Uzbek security forces use "torture as a routine investigation technique," Washington [in 2003] gave the Karimov regime $500 million in aid and rent payments for the US air base in Khanahad. Though Uzbek Muslims can be arrested simply for wearing a long beard, the State Department also quietly removed Uzbekistan from its annual list of countries where freedom of religion is under threat.

In the Uzbek capital of Tashkent, I once met 20-year-old Ahmad, who declined to give his family name out of fear of reprisal. Over a cup of tea the young man told me that he had just been released from prison, after serving a three-year sentence for allegedly belonging to an Islamic terrorist organization. "The guards beat me every day," Ahmad said, his eyes cast down. "It was awful, but I never stopped praying to Allah."

The group the Muslim belonged to was a religious Sufi order that, he insisted, had nothing to do with terrorists such as the Islamic Movement of Uzbekistan, which is blamed for several deadly attacks in the late 1990s. "But maybe in the future my brothers and I have to defend ourselves and fight," he told me. I asked Ahmad how he felt about the arrival of American antiterror troops in Uzbekistan. "They only make things worse. They don't help us, the people, but only the government. I hate America."

What makes a man a terrorist? On my travels, I met countless angry young men who, with nothing to lose but their seemingly valueless lives, were prepared to fight for whatever radical Islamic leaders told them was worth the fight. As in the Middle East, lack of democracy is one of the root causes of terrorism in Central Asia: The young men's anger is primarily directed against their own corrupt and despotic regimes. As Washington shores up these rulers, their disgusted subjects increasingly embrace militant Islam and virulent anti-Americanism.

The Impact of Oil

Recent events in Azerbaijan are perfect examples of how this works. Whenever I travel to the capital of Baku, I am impressed with the new glittery office buildings in the city center and the many flashy Mercedes cars on the streets. Smart biznizmeny [businessmen] and their wives stroll past expensive boutiques, wearing Versace and Cartier jewelry. They are the few winners of the oil boom. Just ten miles out of Baku, however, in the desolate suburb of Sumgait, about 50,000 people live in abject poverty. Many are refugees who fled the war between Azerbaijan and Armenia over the Nagorno-Karabakh enclave in the early 1990s.

All of Sumgait's fourteen Soviet-era factories have been shut down, leaving everybody jobless. There is little electricity or running water. One man, who eked out a living with his wife and several children and grandchildren in a single room of a shabby highrise block, told me, "What oil boom? Our president's family and the oil companies put all the money into their pockets."

Azerbaijan is known as "BP country," as the company wields a budget of $15 billion to be invested off the Azeri coast over the coming years. "If we pulled out of Baku," a former BP spokesman once told me, "the country would collapse overnight." So Big Oil's interests had to be taken into account when Azerbaijan's late ruler, Heydar Aliyev, feeling that his death was nigh, rigged the presidential elections [in] October [2003] to pass on his crown to his playboy son Ilham. This establishment of the first dynasty in the former Soviet Union triggered popular protests in the capital that were brutally put down by Aliyev's security forces. They arrested hundreds of opposition members and killed at least two people.

The next day, US Deputy Secretary of State Richard Armitage officially congratulated the new baby dictator on his "strong showing." Armitage is also a former board member of the US-Azerbaijan Chamber of Commerce in Washington, set up in 1995 to promote US companies' interests in Azerbaijan's multibillion-dollar oil industry. Democracy versus stability for oil investments—few Azeris will forget what side the US government took.

It need not be that way. The US-supported overthrow in November [2003] of strongman Eduard Shevardnadze in neighboring Georgia, a linchpin country for the pipeline export of Caspian oil and gas, showed that protecting strategic energy interests can, however accidentally, go hand in hand with promoting democracy. To be sure, the Bush Administration's motives for dropping Shevardnadze had less to do with a sudden pro-democracy epiphany than with hardnosed realpolitik: Washington's longtime pet ally—who had secured nearly $100 million in annual US aid for Georgia, which is more per capita than any other country except Israel—could no longer provide stability in Georgia and had recently allowed Russian companies to buy up most of the country's energy sector, which increased Moscow's clout on this crucial Great Game battleground at Washington's expense.

"It's All About Oil"

While it is too early to tell how things in Georgia will play out, one general lesson appears clear: The September 11 attacks have shown that the US government can no longer afford to be indifferent toward how badly dictators in the Middle East and Central Asia treat their people, as long as they keep the oil flowing. American dealings with Saudi Arabia have become a fatal affair. President Bush acknowledged as much in recent speeches calling on Saudi Arabia to start democratic reforms to dry up the breeding ground for terrorism.

In Central Asia, however, the current US policy of aiding tyrants repeats the very same mistakes that gave rise to bin Ladenism in the 1980s and '90s. Most Central Asians believe that US antiterror troops are stationed in their region mainly to secure American oil interests. I lost count of how many Azeris, Uzbeks, Afghans and Iraqis I met during my travels who told me that "it's all about oil." Right or wrong, this distrust of the US government's motives is one of the key factors in the insurgencies in Afghanistan and Iraq. The presence of US troops on their soil motivates angry Muslim men to sign up with Al Qaeda–like terror groups. However terribly they suffered under Saddam Hussein, few Iraqis today believe that America would have sent its young men and women to the region if there were only strawberry fields to protect.

With or without military force, there are obvious limits to any US government's ability to nudge autocratic petrostate regimes toward democratic reform—especially as long as America is becoming ever more dependent on oil imports. An addict is hardly able to force his pusher to change his criminal activities. In the United States, 4 percent of the world's population consumes one-fourth of the world's energy. One out of every seven barrels of oil produced in the world is burned on American highways. This is not quite a position that allows us to tell Arab oil sheiks and Central Asian despots, "If you don't stop churning out angry young men, we won't do business with you anymore."

The Need to Reduce Dependence on Oil

For the common people in all oil-producing countries (except Norway and Britain), oil wealth has been more of a curse than a blessing, leading to corruption, political instability, economic decline, environmental degradation, coups and often bloody civil wars. This is why oil is known as the "devil's tears." Today, however, the local people's problems are America's too, because it has become clear since the September 11 attacks how the politics of oil contribute to the rise of radical Islamic terrorism.

So, while the war on terror may not be all about oil, certainly in one sense it should be about just that. A bold policy to reduce the addiction to oil would be the most powerful weapon to win the epic struggle against terrorism. In the short term, this means saving energy through more efficient technologies, necessary anyway to slow the greenhouse effect and global warming. The Bush Administration's old-style energy policies of yet more fossil-fuel production and waste continue in the wrong direction. It is time to realize that more gas-guzzling Hummers on US highways only lead to more Humvees (and American soldiers) near oilfields. What is urgently needed instead—for security reasons—is a sustainable alternative energy policy.

Ultimately, no matter how cleverly the United States plays its cards in the new Great Game in Central Asia and no matter how many military forces are deployed to protect oilfields and pipelines, the oil infrastructure may prove too vulnerable to terrorist attacks to guarantee a stable supply. The Caspian region may be the next big gas station, but, as in the Middle East, there are already a lot of men running around throwing matches.

Periodical Bibliography

The following articles have been selected to supplement the diverse views presented in this chapter.

Gawdat Bahgat	"Oil and Militant Islam: Strains on U.S.-Saudi Relations," *World Affairs*, Winter 2003.
Donald L. Bartlett and James B. Steele	"The Oily Americans: Why the World Doesn't Trust the U.S. About Petroleum," *Time*, May 19, 2003.
Robert Dreyfuss	"The Thirty-Year Itch: For Three Decades, Washington's Hawks Have Pushed for the United States to Seize Control of the Persian Gulf. Their Time Is Now," *Mother Jones*, March/April 2003.
Donald F. Hepburn	"Is It a War for Oil?" *Middle East Policy*, Spring 2003.
Bob Herbert	"Oil and Blood," *New York Times*, July 28, 2005.
Michael T. Klare	"American Military Serves as a Global Oil-Protection Service," *Human Quest*, November/December 2004.
Jehangir Pocha	"The Axis of Oil," *In These Times*, February 28, 2005.
William Schneider	"War Has Its Reasons," *National Journal*, March 22, 2003.
Jonathan Tepperman	"Our Oil Policy Isn't Immoral," *Los Angeles Times*, April 29, 2004.
Matthew Yeomans	"Crude Politics: The United States, China, and the Race for Oil Security," *Atlantic Monthly*, April 2005.
John Zogby	"A War for Hearts and Minds: Most People in the Middle East Think the Iraq War Is About Oil," *New Scientist*, April 5, 2003.

For Further Discussion

Chapter 1

1. Colin J. Campbell asserts that the world's oil supplies are running out, while M.A. Adelman contends that this is not the case. Based on your reading of these viewpoints, do you believe that the world's oil supplies are nearing depletion? Support your answer with examples from the viewpoints.

2. Paul Roberts and Dennis Behreandt disagree over whether or not the United States faces an energy crisis. What points might these two authors agree on, however? Explain your answer.

3. Three of the authors in chapter one believe a worldwide oil crisis is approaching while three of the authors believe that fear of an oil crisis is exaggerated. After reading this chapter, do you think the world faces an oil crisis in the future? Cite from the texts to back up your position.

Chapter 2

1. List four pieces of evidence that Jerry Taylor and Peter Van Doren offer to support their argument that America does not need more oil refineries. In your opinion, which of these is the most convincing? Which is the least convincing? Explain.

2. Walter J. Hickel and Elizabeth Kolbert disagree on whether or not drilling for oil should be allowed in Alaska's Arctic National Wildlife Refuge. Based on your reading of these viewpoints, would you support a proposal to allow drilling there? Explain, quoting from the texts to back up your answer.

3. The authors in chapter two offer various theories about what causes high gas prices in the United States. After reading this chapter, what do you think is the most important factor driving America's gas prices? Explain, citing from the text to support your position.

Chapter 3

1. Joan Claybrook argues that the United States should raise its Corporate Average Fuel Economy (CAFE) standards in order to reduce its dependence on oil. David N. Laband and Christopher Westley contend that such a policy would be dangerous. In your opinion, would higher CAFE standards be harmful or beneficial to the United States? Explain.

2. Douglas L. Faulkner claims that America is on the way to achieving a hydrogen economy. David Morris insists that a hydrogen economy is not the solution to America's energy problems. After reading these viewpoints, do you believe the U.S. government should continue to invest in the development of hydrogen as an energy source? What might be the benefits of such a policy? What are the possible disadvantages of investing in hydrogen?

3. In 2005 the U.S. government passed an energy bill designed to solve some of the energy problems that the country faces. Samuel Bodman claims that the bill will be successful; however, the *Sarasota Herald Tribune* argues that the bill does not effectively address America's energy problems. Do you believe the 2005 energy bill is an effective piece of legislation? Back up your answers by quoting from the viewpoints.

Chapter 4

1. America's involvement in the 2003 Iraq War was motivated by the need for oil, according to Paul Rogers. On

the other hand, Charles A. Kohlhaas argues against this claim, noting that invading Iraq to control its oil would have been an extremely bad business decision. Based on your reading of the viewpoints, which argument do you think is stronger? Why?

2. Joe Barnes, Amy Jaffe, Edward L. Morse, and Robert Mc-Garvey discuss America's dependence on oil from the Middle East. On what points do they agree? On what points do they differ? Which viewpoint most strongly influences your opinion on what policy the United States should pursue regarding oil imports from the Middle East? Why?

3. Irwin M. Stelzer, Joseph Braude, and Lutz Kleveman all make different arguments about how oil influences global politics. In your opinion, how might international relations change if the world was no longer dependent on oil for energy? Explain, citing from the viewpoints to support your answer.

Organizations to Contact

American Petroleum Institute (API)
1220 L St. NW, Washington, DC 20005
(202) 682-8000
Web site: www.api.org

The American Petroleum Institute is a trade association representing America's petroleum industry. Its activities include lobbying, conducting research, and setting technical standards for the petroleum industry. API publishes numerous position papers, reports, and information sheets.

American Solar Energy Society (ASES)
2400 Central Ave., Suite A
  Boulder, CO 80301
(303) 443-3130
Web site: www.ases.org

ASES promotes widespread near-term and long-term use of solar energy. It organizes the National Solar Energy Conference, the National Solar Tour, and publishes *Solar Today* magazine.

American Wind Energy Association (AWEA)
1101 Fourteenth St. NW, 12th Fl.
  Washington, DC 20005
(202) 383-2500 • fax: (202) 383-2505
Web site: www.awea.org

Since 1974 the AWEA has advocated the development of wind energy as a reliable, environmentally superior energy alternative in the United States and around the world. Its publications include the *AWEA Wind Energy Weekly* and the monthly *Windletter*.

Brookings Institution
1775 Massachusetts Ave. NW, Washington, DC 20036
(202) 797-6000 • fax: (202) 797-6004
e-mail: brookinfo@brook.edu
Web site: www.brookings.org

The Brookings Institution is a private, nonprofit organization that conducts research on economics, education, foreign and domestic government policy, and the social sciences. In articles published by the institute in its quarterly journal, *Brookings Review*, researchers and scholars have taken the position that free-market forces, not military intervention, should form the basis of U.S. energy policy. Brookings also publishes several energy-related books.

Cato Institute
1000 Massachusetts Ave. NW
    Washington, DC 20001
(202) 842-0200 • fax (202) 842-3490
e-mail: cato@cato.org
Web site: www.cato.org

The Cato Institute is a libertarian public policy research foundation dedicated to limiting the role of government and promoting individual liberty. It disapproves of spending taxpayer funds to intervene in the political affairs of oil-producing countries, arguing that the world oil market will respond evenly to the forces of supply and demand and preclude oil shortages. The institute publishes the quarterly magazine *Regulation*, and the bimonthly *Cato Policy Report*, both of which have featured articles critical of U.S. foreign policy as it pertains to oil in the Middle East.

Competitive Enterprise Institute (CEI)
1001 Connecticut Ave. NW, Suite 1250
    Washington, DC 20036
(202) 331-1010 • fax: (202) 331-0640
e-mail: info@cei.org
Web site: www.cei.org

CEI is a nonprofit public policy organization dedicated to the principles of free enterprise and limited government. The institute advocates removing government environmental regulations to establish a system in which the private sector is responsible for energy policy. CEI's publications include the newsletter *Monthly Planet, On Point* policy briefs, and the books *Global Warming and Other Eco-Myths* and *The True State of the Planet.*

Council on Alternative Fuels (CAF)
1225 I St. NW, Suite 320
   Washington, DC 20005
(202) 898-0711

CAF comprises companies interested in the production of synthetic fuels and the research and development of synthetic fuel technology. It publishes information on new alternative fuels in the monthly *Alternative Fuel News.*

Heritage Foundation
214 Massachusetts Ave. NE
   Washington, DC 20002
(202) 546-4400 • fax: (202) 546-8328
Web site: www.heritage.org

The Heritage Foundation is a conservative public policy think tank that advocates an increase in U.S. oil production. Its publications include the quarterly journal *Policy Review*, brief "Executive Memorandum" editorials, and the longer Backgrounder series of studies.

International Association for Hydrogen Energy (IAHE)
PO Box 248266
   Coral Gables, FL 33124
(305) 284-4666
Web site: www.iahe.org

The IAHE is a group of scientists and engineers professionally involved in the production and use of hydrogen. It sponsors international forums to further its goal of creating an energy system based on hydrogen. The IAHE publishes the monthly *International Journal for Hydrogen Energy.*

Reason Public Policy Institute (RPPI)
3415 S. Sepulveda Blvd., Suite 400
  Los Angeles, CA 90034
(310) 391-2245 • fax: (310) 391-4395
e-mail: feedback@reason.org
Web site: www.rppi.org

RPPI is a research organization that supports less government interference in the lives of Americans. Its libertarian philosophy stands firmly opposed to raising the fuel economy standards of automobiles, arguing that doing so will necessitate smaller cars and thus result in more fatal traffic accidents. The institute publishes the monthly magazine *Reason*.

Renewable Fuels Association (RFA)
1 Massachusetts Ave. NW, Suite 820
  Washington, DC 20001
(202) 289-3835 • fax: (202) 289-7519
e-mail: info@ethanolrfa.org
Web site: www.ethanolrfa.org

RFA comprises professionals who research, produce, and market renewable fuels, especially alcohol fuels. It also represents the renewable fuels industry before the federal government. RFA publishes the monthly newsletter *Ethanol Report*.

Worldwatch Institute
1776 Massachusetts Ave. NW
  Washington, DC 20036-1904
(202) 452-1999 • fax: (202) 296-7365
e-mail: worldwatch@worldwatch.org
Web site: www.worldwatch.org

Worldwatch is a nonprofit public policy research organization dedicated to informing policy makers and the public about emerging global problems and the complex links between the world economy and its environmental support systems. The institute takes the position that the U.S. government should not engage in wars for the sake of securing a steady oil supply,

and it maintains that alternative energies need accelerated research and government support. It publishes the bimonthly
World Watch magazine, the Environmental Alert series, and
numerous policy papers.

Bibliography of Books

Godfrey Boyle — *Renewable Energy.* New York: Oxford University Press, 2004.

Julian Darley — *High Noon for Natural Gas: The New Energy Crisis.* White River Junction, VT: Chelsea Green, 2004.

Kristen A. Day, ed. — *China's Environment and the Challenge of Sustainable Development.* Armonk, NY: M.E. Sharpe, 2005.

Kenneth S. Deffeyes — *Beyond Oil: The View from Hubbert's Peak.* New York: Hill and Wang, 2005.

Kenneth S. Deffeyes — *Hubbert's Peak: The Impending World Oil Shortage.* Princeton, NJ: Princeton University Press, 2003.

Emirates Center for Strategic Studies and Research — *Gulf Energy and the World: Challenges and Threats.* London: I.B. Tauris, 2003.

Bob Everett, Godfrey Boyle, and Janet Ramage — *Energy Systems and Sustainability.* New York: Oxford University Press, 2003.

Howard Geller — *Energy Revolution: Policies for a Sustainable Future.* Washington, DC: Island Press, 2003.

David L. Goodstein — *Out of Gas: The End of the Age of Oil.* New York: Norton, 2004.

Richard Heinberg   *The Party's Over: Oil, War, and the Fate of Industrial Society.* Gabriola, BC: New Society, 2003.

Peter W. Huber   *The Bottomless Well: The Twilight of Fuel, the Virtue of Waste, and Why We Will Never Run Out of Energy.* New York: Basic Books, 2005.

Michael T. Klare   *Blood and Oil: The Dangers and Consequences of America's Growing Petroleum Dependency.* New York: Metropolitan/Henry Holt, 2004.

James Howard Kunstler   *The Long Emergency: Surviving the Converging Catastrophes of the Twenty-First Century.* New York: Atlantic Monthly, 2005.

Barbara E. Ornitz and Michael A. Champ   *Oil Spills: First Principles; Prevention and Best Response.* New York: Elsevier, 2002.

Paul Roberts   *The End of Oil: On the Edge of a Perilous New World.* New York: Houghton Mifflin, 2004.

Hermann Scheer   *The Solar Economy: Renewable Energy for a Sustainable Global Future.* London: Earthscan, 2004.

Matthew R. Simmons   *Twilight in the Desert: The Coming Saudi Oil Shock and the World Economy.* Hoboken, NJ: John Wiley & Sons, 2005.

U.S. Congress, House Committee on International Relations — *Oil Diplomacy: Facts and Myths Behind Foreign Oil Dependency*, 107th Cong., 2nd Sess., 2002.

Charles Woolfson and Matthias Beck, eds. — *Corporate Social Responsibility Failures in the Oil Industry*. Amityville, NY: Baywood, 2005.

Matthew Yeomans — *Oil: Anatomy of an Industry*. New York: New Press, 2004.

Index